Culturally Responsive Educational Theories:
A Practical Guide with Case Studies for Improving the Academic Performance of Diverse Learners

Dr. Tyrone Tanner

ISBN   (978-0-9834914-3-9) - perfect bound
          (978-0-9834914-4-6) - case bound
          (978-0-9834914-5-3) - ebook

Library of Congress Control Number: 2013932430

Educational Concepts, LLC
12320 Barker Cypress Road
Suite 600-111
Cypress, TX 77429
www.educationalconcepts4you.com
info@educationalconcepts4you.com
Phone (888) 630-6650
Fax: (877) 310-6692

Cover and interior layout by Perfectly Frank Papers
(www.perfectlyfrankpapers.com)

First Edition
First Printing February 2013

Ordering Information:
Quantity Sales: Special discounts are available on quantities purchased by corporations, associations, school districts, and others.
Individual Sales: Educational Concepts publications can be ordered directly from the publisher or from most bookstores.
Orders for College Textbook/Course Adoption Use: Please contact Educational Concepts, LLC directly.

DEDICATION

This book is dedicated to every educator across the nation,
and the students, who are depending on your success.

TABLE OF CONTENTS

FOREWORD
BY DR. NORVELLA CARTER

When I was a child in the 1950s, it was clearly communicated to me, as an African American, that education was the key to a quality life and the survival of future generations. It was also conveyed that we were not yet equal to European Americans because we were subjected to an inferior educational system. As research has revealed, the myth of the struggles of African American students and other diverse populations has nothing to do with race but, with the need to be educated by a culturally responsive educator. Today, through the sacrifices of parents, educators, civil rights and community leaders, millions of educated diverse learners have now attained the illusive dream of an education. Yet, the struggle to educate children of color in mass has not changed; meaning, there is still much that needs to be continued, as the achievement gap is still pervasive.

Dr. Tyrone Tanner, in this work, elaborates on the struggles by describing how culturally responsive educational theories address the needs of our children by targeting the views of the teacher, often unbeknownst to them. Current research on diverse learners reveals that inadequate access to and receipt of quality instruction in general education and special education environments are significant factors contributing to this *struggling* phenomenon. Simply put, effectively teaching diverse learners is a monumental challenge for teachers and educators, who fail to understand the socialized cultural strengths and cultural contexts experienced by youth. It is vividly apparent that the author's mission is to assist educators in adopting culturally responsive educational theories and practices for the purpose of improving educational service delivery and outcomes for all learners.

The author cites low teacher efficacy and locus of control as factors contributing to the academic struggles of children. In this book, Dr. Tanner, using scholarly research, describes ways children's education are hindered by a lack of knowledge by teachers, who expect so little of them and exhibit such low expectations, that the students' academic performance is obstructed. The author provides a vivid picture of ways teachers' expectations enter the lives of our children early on to relegate them to paths of low-level instruction and sometimes, unwarranted special education. As educators, we are aware of the over representation of diverse children in special education and their under-representation in honors and advanced placement classes. Dr. Tanner gives voice to this lament. Not since Cornel West's book, *Race Matters*, has an author provided such a descriptive view of how and why children have been impacted by low expectations and powerful views that influenced the learning outcomes of diverse learners.

Dr. Tanner's poignant chapter on Critical Race Theory sets forth a riveting description of how some teachers use race to prohibit the success of students of color in school. He cites too many teachers as having a low sense of teacher efficacy, based on the race of the students, and promotes the need for our teachers to be prepared to teach *all* children in our diverse society. The case studies that Dr. Tanner shares are most revealing. He provides rich descriptions by using the actual words of those involved in the scenarios. His work is profound, as he shares the lived experiences of students and teachers. Often, readers will encounter the work of writers, who tell gripping stories that end in despair and hopelessness. Although many of the experiences of the students are painful, Dr. Tanner does not leave the reader hanging in despair. Through his characteristic of being an empowered educator, he gives an injection of hope for the future. Readers of this work will be able to reflect on its contents and conclude that it gives voice to those, who struggle in our educational system. In addition, Dr. Tanner provides insight on the lessons learned in his scenarios. He stresses the pursuit of high achievement in the midst of struggle and offers strategic solutions for educating children in diverse classrooms. Dr. Tyrone Tanner, a champion for students and an activist for the progressive movement of education, is applauded for providing a practical guide for improving the academic performance of diverse learners. His insightful work will be beneficial to parents, educators, political leaders and those interested in the education of diverse learners.

Norvella Carter, Ph.D.
Endowed Chair in Urban Education
Texas A&M University, College Station

PREFACE

This book is firmly grounded in the belief that all students can learn and use education as a tool for personal, social, and economic mobility. When students are provided a classroom environment, which supports the use of culturally responsive teaching strategies, students can learn exceptionally well. In addition, I support the theoretical notion that thoroughly prepared, culturally responsive educators are able to provide equitable opportunities in which all learners will achieve success. My teaching, research, and service activities seek to provide educators with the tools necessary for all students, particularly children of color, to experience academic and life success.

Although my philosophy is evidenced in this book, it is my first-hand experiences, as an African-American male in the public school system, that have influenced and formed my philosophy and, as a result, the content in this book. As a product of both the urban and rural K-12 public educational systems, I was exposed to schools and educators, who failed to understand students representing diverse populations and their cultures. I experienced classrooms, which were not culturally responsive, and, unfortunately, I did not thrive academically. As a young, energetic, third-grade male, I found myself trying to create excitement in, what I deemed, a boring classroom. These actions, earned me the label, "troublemaker." This label afforded me multiple trips to the principal's office. After two years of living in the principal's office and earning a well-established reputation as a mischievous child, I was assigned to an "angel" of a teacher, Ms. McDuffie. Ms. McDuffie displayed characteristics of a culturally responsive teacher and created a culturally responsive classroom. Through this relationship, Ms. McDuffie created a sense of responsibility in me. My label changed from "troublemaker" to "Super Star." I began to thrive academically. Although I had not changed, I was still the same young, active, busy, little boy, my environment had changed. I had a teacher, who was responsive to my individual needs. She created a culture in which I experienced success. As a self-efficacious teacher possessing high expectations, Ms. McDuffie supported and encouraged me to strive to master the reading and math curriculum. Through frequent tutoring sessions, she observed my "giftedness." As a result, I was identified as one of seven students, from a pool of over 500, who qualified for the most competitive gifted programs in the city. Through her culturally responsive practices, Ms. McDuffie motivated me to reach my full potential. She identified and saw potential that no one else was able to see. Her belief in me became my demonstrated reality.

These experiences began to shape my teaching philosophy, first from my experiences as a student of color in the public school system and, ultimately, as an educator. My research and my personal experiences support the philosophy that students can and will achieve when provided a culturally responsive environment. I firmly believe in this philosophical approach and support educators seeking to build classrooms in which all students can and do experience phenomenal academic success. Sadly, youth of color are often exposed to an educational system focusing on students' deficits, rather than developing their strengths and resiliency. Culturally responsive classrooms support student resiliency and students' potentials.

Over the last 20 years, I've worked with various school districts to assist their students in overcoming the barriers, which often get in the way of great teaching and student success. I believe in helping educators unwrap themselves, while challenging them to view difficult, challenging, and/or unmotivated students from a different perspective. This process is incredibly powerful since our minds have a responsibility to find the evidence to support our views and perspectives.

In this book, we seek to challenge the views of educators, which often get in the way of learners experiencing success. For example, as an educator, if you have never taught an African American child, who was a mathematical genius, or an Asian American, who struggled academically, your interpretation may be getting in the way of creating the desired outcome. Until we have the encounters necessary to create the shifts in our thinking or views, we will continue to find the evidence to support our views. Hence, we will continue experiencing the same outcomes. Unless educators' perspectives change, students of color will fail to reach their full potential.

In the following chapters, we will focus on sharing the empowering foundations, necessary to experience success with our learners. Educators are trained in ways that tap their self-efficacy and internal locus of control as well as procure information regarding the learning styles of the students with which they struggle the most.

My personal life experiences, along with the mentorship of scholars like Drs. Norvella Carter, Gwen Webb-Johnson Hasaan, Cherry Gooden, Chance Lewis, and Leetta-Allen Haynes, have contributed to the formation of my philosophical approach.

My philosophy, as reflected in this book, seeks to critically examine and help educators develop an awareness of classrooms, which are unresponsive to student needs. Teaching, training, and impacting educators, to be equipped with the tools and self-efficacy necessary to successfully transform classrooms and campuses so that no student is left behind, is the foundation of this book. This is also my approach toward equipping educators to serve the leaders of tomorrow.

To Drs. Douglas Hermond, Queinnise Miller, and Max Fontus, thank you for your partnership with me in developing a powerful and unique Culturally Responsive Identification Instrument. This instrument is groundbreaking and will make a difference in quickly identifying culturally responsive educators, and the specific culturally responsive tools educators need to experience success with all learners, specifically diverse learners.

In addition, I would like to acknowledge my mother, who has been a teacher for 56 years, and continues to advocate that every student has a "right" to a quality education and teacher. To my sister, Angela, for being like a second mother. Thank you for your friendship. To my brother, Forrest, thank you for modeling the importance of learning and the consistent message of "effort equals outcome." Finally, to my wife, Chrysaundra, thank you for your love and support. And to my children, thank you for being so loving. I'm the proudest father in the world. With every book I write or presentation I share, I think of you first. You are my inspiration.

Tyrone Tanner
January 15, 2013

CONTRIBUTORS

I would like to acknowledge and extend my heartfelt gratitude to the following contributors, who made the completion of this project possible: Dr. Norvella Carter, for her vital encouragement and support. Specifically, thank you for the poignant foreword you wrote for this book.

To Latoya Mills, thank you for allowing me to share your creativity through the amazing Symbolic Interactions case study. Perfectly Frank Papers, Dr. Vickie Moon Merchant, Dr. Lisa K. Thompson and Dr. Lisa Hobson, thank you for your timely and professional editorial services. Many thanks also to my doctoral students, for sharing your ideas and thoughts on ways to make our education system stronger. Most especially, I would like to thank my family and friends for your support, and to God, who makes all things possible.

CHAPTER 1
Introduction

The authors of this book seek to share explanations, which get in the way of learning, while creating extraordinary learning in the classroom. Uniquely, both a practitioner and a researcher wrote this book. Hence, the layout of the book includes answers and solutions to relevant questions like, "Why don't my students' parents trust me?" or "Why do my students' parents keep blaming me for their student's failure?" The first step to understanding where distrust begins is the first step to removing it. This book provides the steps of understanding, through clear explanations of ways students learn and process information. Other questions to be answered include: "Why is one student motivated by the teacher having lunch with them, while others are motivated by the grades they earn?" or "Why do some students excel in one teacher's class and struggle in another's?" Again, the authors provide both the explanations and solutions to these common questions.

For the teacher, the book provides a powerful understanding of the importance of our perspectives and biases and how our minds automatically seek the evidence to support our views. Most importantly, we discuss the importance of shifting our views, when necessary, for the students to experience optimal success, as discussed in Chapter 4, The Pygmalion Effect of this book. We also address common misconceptions individuals have with words, such as culture and ethnicity. For example, culture is socially transmitted, it changes and it is fluid. Culture can't be race and vice versa. Who I am, from an ethnic standpoint, will always be who I am, but my culture can change. You can be part of a culture of low expectations and create a culture of high expectations, as culture is fluid. You can be born into a culture of poverty and rise out of that to become successful and wealthy.

Culture is very separate from race. Race was created as a false classification system for the sole purpose of creating a superior and inferior group of people. That is the purpose of race; otherwise we would all just be human beings. Unfortunately, the definition of culture has been confused with race. Because of this, assumptions are made due to a person's skin color or language skills. These assumptions often create a barrier against certain groups; thereby, hindering their ability to thrive and succeed in mainstream education.

Often I hear that children are not experiencing success because they come from a culture of poverty. Interestingly, countless schools across the United States are experiencing academic success with students, who come from that same demographic. A more important question would be; if we really believe that poverty is the issue, why don't we control for it? The Critical Race Theory discussed in Chapter 3 provides insight into this question. Furthering this discussion, if we go internationally, Cuba is one of the most financially poor countries in the world; yet, they are one of the most literate. As we have seen in the United States and other countries abroad, poverty is not the issue but, teacher preparation and education. All educational preparation programs must do a better job of preparing educators for the learners they serve and ways they learn.

Lastly, this book is an attempt to clarify the many theories that exist with regard to being culturally responsive. The goal is to help you, as an educator or just an interested human being, understand the underlying reasons behind much of the "culture of low expectations" or the "culture of failure" prevalent in our schools. It is through deeper understanding of how children learn, process information, internalize experiences, and react to situations, that we can more effectively teach them and help *all* students to succeed. As an added bonus, after each theory, case studies are provided to reinforce the concepts of the theory.

CHAPTER 2
Cultural Ecology

Theoretical Framework

One explanation for the success or failure of students of color appears to be found in John Ogbu's (1981) theory of *Cultural Ecology*. Ogbu's (1981) theory considers the broad societal and educational factors, as well as the dynamics within the community of the student of color (Ogbu & Simon, 1998). Cultural refers to the way people see their world and behave in it, while ecology is defined as the setting, environment, or world in which people live, (Ogbu & Simon, 1998). For over twenty years, John Ogbu conducted research on reasons some groups become successful, while others struggled.

Ogbu's analysis focused on two types of forces influencing school behavior of students' of color. The nature of the history and exploitation experienced by the people of the under-served population was regarded as the first force (Gibson, 1997). This included the manner in which the group was initially introduced into the mainstream society. The second force noted the nature of the adaptive response to the discriminatory treatment, which people of color experienced (Gibson, 1997).

Based on Ogbu's theory, people arrived in their host country through voluntary or involuntary means (Ogbu, 1991). Voluntary minorities were described as immigrants, who choose to come to a country believing they would obtain greater political freedom or financial gain. In essence, they believed the move to another country would improve their quality of life. According to Ogbu (1987), because voluntary immigrants choose to begin a new life in a different country, they felt obligated to assimilate into the new society and assume responsibility for overcoming language and other barriers. They believe these obstacles to be temporary and part of the price to be paid in order to be successful in the host country (Ogbu, 1991). Therefore, voluntary immigrants mentally compared their past situations and future possibilities with those they might have experienced in their homeland.

According to Ogbu (1991), groups such as Chinese immigrants (voluntary) often arrived in America believing their families' lives would greatly improve as a result of immigrating to the United States. However, this optimistic perspective, along with the belief in the folk theory of success, which claimed education and hard work were the keys to social mobility, combined to impact academic achievement. In addition, their belief that obstacles temporarily assisted Chinese immigrants in accepting responsibility for overcoming barriers, also influenced academic achievement. Finally, this 'dual frame of reference' aided them in positively comparing their current status to what it could have been in their homeland (Ogbu, 1987). Currently, Chinese Americans are one of the immigrant groups in America experiencing the greatest academic success.

In contrast, involuntary immigrants were conquered, colonized or enslaved and were brought to a different country against their will (Ogbu, 1987). Because involuntary people of color were forced and did not choose to come to America, they were less optimistic and believed discriminatory barriers were fixed. As a result, involuntary immigrants often developed an oppositional identity and distrust of the mainstream population and of the established and controlled institutions they created (Ogbu, 1987). Ogbu (1991) argued the way an immigrant group was incorporated into society influenced how they would respond to the discriminatory barriers experienced. These responses shaped voluntary and involuntary immigrants' cultural models, which impacted the attitudes and motivation students of color brought to the classroom.

On the contrary, Ogbu (1991) stated African-Americans, as involuntary immigrants, often exemplified distrust of established institutions, such as education, controlled by the mainstream population. Because people in power controlled these institutions, discriminatory practices were established and institutional barriers were created. These barriers were viewed as fixed and aided involuntary immigrants in developing an oppositional identity to mainstream values (Ogbu, 1991).

Ogbu (1978) found similar results in six countries: Britain, India, Israel, Japan, New Zealand, and the United States. In each country, his study dealt with the education of caste-like people of color. He classified the minorities as caste-like because in every case they were a subordinate group in a stratified system, more rigid than social class stratification (Ogbu, 1978). In every case, the people representing minority populations historically were denied equal educational opportunities in terms of access to educational resources, supervision in schools, rewards in employment, and wages earned based on educational accomplishments (Ogbu, 1978). Ogbu concluded academic performance was an adaptation to barriers in adult opportunity structures (Ogbu, 1978). He suggested his findings transcend social economic status, stating affluent African-American students in suburban school districts, as well as poor African-Americans in inner city schools, were unsuccessful due to factors rooted in both the school systems and communities (Ogbu, 2003).

Ogbu (1987) recognized that not all voluntary immigrants were academically successful and that not all involuntary minorities were unsuccessful. However, he argued the cultural model of immigrants' arrival in their new country influenced the development of attitudes and strategies that facilitate or hinder academic success (Ogbu, 1987).

Other education scholars acknowledged Ogbu's *Cultural Ecology Theory* (1981); however, they fail to accept his theory as conclusive. They stressed that resistance from students of color could not only come from a group's history but, also from experiencing alienating teaching procedures within the schools (Foley, 1991; Trueba & Zou, 1994). Further, they posited Ogbu's position left no room for the possible impact of school change (Foley, 1991; Trueba & Zou, 1994).

Implications for Education

The theory and reality of *Cultural Ecology* appears to have severe implications in the ways individuals and their families interact with the U. S. educational system. The impact of interactions is vastly different depending on whether the immigrant group is voluntary or involuntary. Voluntary immigrant groups often display greater trust in the national educational system, which can lead to lack of communication between parents and school staff unless initiated by the latter. Parents, who are voluntary immigrants, tend to often assume that the 'system' is taking care of their child and that if they ask questions, it may show their lack of trust in the schools. Teachers and school administrators should be mindful as they interact with these parents and their students. Increased school-initiated communication is essential in ensuring that the trust in not misplaced and the parent is fully aware of the events occurring in the school setting.

Involuntary immigrants are much more likely to display distrust of the educational system. These parents tend to question the motives of teachers and administrators. Often parents' assumptions and feelings of distrust are based on prior experiences occurring within the schools. Often school officials respond to the distrust negatively, a natural human response. Nonetheless, failure to become aware of this theory often results in school officials increasing distrust. For the aforementioned reasons, teachers and administrators should make an intentional effort to make these families feel that they are essential in the educational process of their students through building trust. Later, we will discuss additional theories that, when combined with *Cultural Ecology*, provide explanations of the approaches to be considered. For school officials, being cognizant of these obstacles and having a plan in place to combat them, is imperative.

Statistical evidence of this distrust is also present when we examine the demographics of student population in higher education. For example, the number of Native American students, who enroll in a post-secondary educational program, is extremely low even though many have access to a free college education. In 2010, the National Center for Education Statistics (NCES) reported that out of the total number of Native American students between the ages of 18 and 24, only 28.3% of them were enrolled in college or graduate school. This is compared to 46.9% of Caucasian students and 66% of Asian American students (NCES, 2010). If Native American students experienced culturally responsive pedagogical practices in the K-12 classrooms, their experiences in and likelihood of earning a post-secondary degree might be drastically altered.

Summary of Cultural Ecology

The following table summarizes the characteristics of each immigrant group:

	Voluntary	Involuntary
Characteristics	Trust of system	Distrustful of system
	Dual (home) frame of reference	No dual frame of reference
	Optimistic	Oppositional identity toward mainstream established and controlled institutions
	Believe barriers are temporary	Believe barriers are fixed
Steps Schools Should Take	Consistent communication with parents	Consistent communication with parents
	Increased explanations of systems	Respectful collaboration showing desire for input from parents
	Administrative monitoring of systems to ensure input from all stakeholders	Diversity/cultural awareness training with teaching skills to overcome barriers of distrust for the present system

Case Study 1
Cultural Ecology

As the assistant principal of a high school, Mr. Barr was confronted by a Caucasian student, Isaac, who asked to be transferred to a different high school. Isaac felt that he would have better opportunities in a different high school, where he would have an assistant principal of his own race.

Isaac felt that Mr. Barr always defended African American students because whenever Caucasian students had problems and concerns, their needs were ignored. Isaac believed because of Mr. Barr's inactions, Caucasians were often suspended from school.

In the neighborhood served by the school, tension existed between the African American and Caucasian groups as a result of recurring issues of hatred between these two groups.

Mr. Barr asked Isaac if he could give any example in which he felt he was treated wrongly. Isaac said that he had heard that Mr. Barr sent his Caucasian friend to the Alternative Learning Center (ALC) but, not a African American student who had acted the same way.

Mr. Barr responded by stating, "Each student can have a hearing with their parents to try and reduce the days of ALC or even have them removed." Mr. Barr also told Isaac that sometimes students have been previously disciplined and this additional improper behavior resulted in them being assigned to ALC. Isaac asked how and why his friend had been sent to ALC. Because of confidentiality, Mr. Barr assured Isaac that neither the student's race, nor any prejudice on his part, affected the decision. In this case, the student's parents played an active part in his friend's discipline problems.

Additionally, Mr. Barr asked Isaac to recall anytime when he was treated unfairly in Mr. Barr's office. Mr. Barr mentioned that he had attended football games in which Isaac had played and cheered him to victory. Isaac responded that Mr. Barr had been very encouraging anytime they had been around each other and that he might have misjudged the situation. Then Isaac asked if Mr. Barr could help him with teachers, who had indicated he was missing some assignments. At the conclusion of the discussion, Isaac and Mr. Barr looked at Isaac's progress in each of his classes. Together they decided that Isaac would go to the administrative staff when he had questions or future problems, rather than listening to information from other students.

Questions for Reflection

1. What perception did Isaac have of the assistant principal, Mr. Barr?

2. What environmental factors shaped Isaac's current understanding of culture?

3. What perception does the assistant principal have of himself?

4. What is the difference between listening to friends and listening to authority?

5. What do you think should be the next steps for the building administrator regarding the high school campus?

CASE STUDY
Cultural Ecology

Javon is an African American student, who has been sent to the assistant principal's office for punching another student in the nose. The altercation resulted in the other student suffering a broken nose. When the assistant principal called Javon's mother, her response was, "You all are always picking on my child!"

When the assistant principal explained the situation further, Javon's mother still insisted that her child was being targeted by the administration and that he had been set up to be suspended. Even though the school video system showed that the student had not directly provoked Javon, his mother would not accept the fact that he had caused the problem.

Questions for Reflection

1. In which category, voluntary or involuntary, do Javon and his mother fall?

2. Why do you think Javon's mother responded the way she did to the accusations?

3. What events could have taken place to reinforce her opinion?

4. What, if anything, could the school do to change her opinion?

CASE STUDY
Cultural Ecology

The day was incredibly hot even by Houston, Texas standards. The news reported that the temperature was to reach 100 degrees by 2:00pm. Coach Alexander, the Westview High School physical education teacher, believed that all students should complete the same activities each day regardless of the time of their P. E. class. Every P.E. class began with a run around the track and 20 push-ups on the black top. Daily routines were no different from first period through seventh.

The next day, the school principal, Mr. Hemmings, was walking down the hall and sees Johnny Liu, an Asian American freshman, with his hands completely bandaged. "Johnny!" Mr. Hemmings calls, "What happened to your hands?"

"I spent the night in the hospital last night." Johnny replied, "My hands are all blistered up."

Mr. Hemmings was shocked by this information and immediately went to his office, wondering why he had not gotten a call from the area superintendent or Johnny's parents. He picked up the phone and dialed Johnny's father.

"Mr. Liu, I saw Johnny in the hallway today. I am so sorry about what happened. Please be assured that I am dealing with the situation and will be speaking to the coach immediately."

"Oh, Mr. Hemmings, we know that you have our child's best interests at heart." Mr. Liu responded.

Questions for Reflection

1. How was Mr. Liu's response to Mr. Hemming's different from Javon's mother in the prior case study?

2. Why do you think Mr. Liu responded in the way that he did?

3. What are the dangers of this situation?

4. How can the school ensure that Mr. Liu and his family will continue to trust the system as they do?

REFERENCES

Foley, D. (1991) Reconsidering anthropological explanations of ethnic school failure. *Anthropology and Education Quarterly, 22,* 60–86.

Gibson, (1997). Complicating the immigrant/involuntary minority typology. *Anthropology and Education Quarterly, 28(3),* 431-452.

National Center for Education Statistics. (2010). *Number and percentage of 18 to 24-year-olds in the household and group quarters by population, by school enrollment status, ethnicity and nativity: 2010.* [Data File]. Retrieved from http://nces.ed.gov/pubs2012/2012046/tables/e-33-1.asp

Ogbu, J. U. (1978). *Minority education and caste: The American system in cross-cultural perspective.* New York: Academic Press.

Ogbu, J. U. (1981). School ethnography: A multicultural approach. *Anthropology and Education Quarterly, 12(10),* 3-29.

Ogbu, J. U. (1981). Origins of human competence: A cultural-ecological perspective. *Child Development, 52,* 413-429.

Ogbu, J. U. (1987). Variability in minority school performance: A problem in search of an explanation. *Anthropology and Education Quarterly, 18,* 312-334.

Ogbu, J.U. (2003). *Black American students in an affluent suburb: A study of academic disengagement.* Mahwah, NJ: Lawrence Erlbaum Associates.

Ogbu, J. U., & Simons, H. D. (1998). Voluntary and involuntary minorities: A cultural-ecological theory of school performance with some implications for education. *Anthropology & Education Quarterly, 29(2),* 155-188.

Trueba, H.T., & Zou, Y. (1994). *Power in education: The Miao University students and its significance for American culture.* London: Falmer Press.

CHAPTER 3
Critical Race Theory

Theoretical Framework

Critical race theory aims to challenge conventional accounts of educational and other institutions and the social processes that occur within them. (Powers, 2007, p. 151)

Critical Race Theory (CRT) is a theory born out of the actions of the legal system of the United States in the late 1970s and early 1980s. Members of the legal community and students of law at various institutions around the country witnessed a disparity between the execution of laws for under-served groups, specifically African American and Hispanics, versus the execution of the same laws with respect to members of the majority, or White, population. Critical Race Theory operates on three basic premises: racism is pervasive; racism is permanent; and racism must be challenged (Vaught & Castagno, 2008, p. 96). Critical Race Theory was developed as a way to explain, highlight, and combat the racism that existed, and continues to exist in the United States (Powers, 2007).

Ladson-Billings and Tate (1995) have further developed the Critical Race Theory (CRT) to explain the growing and substantial educational achievement gap existing between European American, or White, students and students of color. Ladson-Billings and Tate (1995) suggested that inequities in school systems from three different propositions: race continues to be a significant factor in determining inequity in America; U.S. society is based primarily on property rights; and the intersection between race and property allows us to understand social and school inequity. Unlike other theories discussed in this book, Critical Race Theory is an idea, or lens, through which educators and policy makers can make sense of the problems currently plaguing the public school system: under-achievement, discipline issues, drop out rates, and others.

> *Most considerations of barriers to educational equality have focused on characteristics of students themselves as the source of the problem. Seen as products of disorganized and deteriorating homes and family structures, poor and minority children have been thought of as unmotivated, noncompetitive and culturally disadvantaged... It turns out that those children, who seem to have the least of everything in the rest of their lives, most often get less at school as well. (Oakes, 2005, p. 4)*

In her acclaimed book, *Keeping Track*, Oakes (2005) outlined the changes that have taken place in the American school system since its inception in the late 1700s. She noted that as immigration began to rapidly increase at the close of the 19th century, America was touted as a melting pot. In reality, the elite ruling class wanted to keep control over the growing immigrant population. This grew from the need to standardize behaviors as the increasing immigrant student population attended overcrowded urban classrooms in which multiple languages were spoken. Thus, new concepts of basic cleanliness, etiquette and behavior crept into the school's curriculum. Thus, the melting pot became a structured Americanization of all immigrants (Oakes, 2005).

Now, even after 100 years, many of the same standards continue to exist even though the ethnic makeup of the country has changed. Systems, established by members of the White, Anglo-Saxon, male ruling population, lack relevance and resonance in today's multicultural populated schools. Critical Race Theory can be applied through changing the discriminatory treatment of African American students with regard to school discipline. This treatment, which is not an isolated phenomenon, appears to be part of a complex inequity associated with special education over-representation, academic placement and achievement, school dropout rate and school funding (Gordon, Piana, & Keleher, 2000).

> Education Trust West (2005) found an average gap of $472,152 per year for funding between schools with a high minority student population and those with a low minority student population. It is believed that by eliminating this financial flaw in the structure, the achievement gap between these two groups of student populations could be closed by 20% to 40%.

These sources of institutional inequity persisting throughout public education do not typically rise to the conscious level, yet they have the effect of reinforcing and perpetuating racial and socioeconomic disadvantages. (Skiba, Michael, Nardo, & Peterson, 2000, p. 18)

Currently, the tenets of Critical Race Theory (CRT) pertain to the following: discipline referrals, special education placement, and academic achievement and will be further examined. Connections will be made between the theory and each area explored, as well as implications for applying CRT to create positive transformations of the areas discussed.

Discipline Referrals

Skiba, Michael, Nardo, and Peterson conducted a comprehensive study in 2000, examining discipline rates and its connection to race, ethnicity and socio-economic status. Their national samples included those schools with predominantly minority populations and those with relatively small minority populations. In their report, *The Color of Discipline: Sources of Racial and Gender Dis-proportionality in School Punishment*, Skiba, Michael, Nardo, and Peterson (2000) outlined the results of their study, as well as the implications. Their findings indicated a disproportionate number of office referrals and suspensions for students of color and those from low socio-economic backgrounds.

A major connection was found between the perceptions of the teachers, the behavior of the students, and the disciplinary reaction. European American teachers appeared to lack understanding of the cultural differences between students of color and themselves. This lack of understanding placed students of color at a disadvantage regarding discipline. Loud, boisterous activity was mistaken for offensive, non-compliance or unruly behavior; thus, students were inaccurately referred to an administrator due to their behavior being seen as a punishable offense (Skiba, Michael, Nardo & Peterson, 2000).

> *The impassioned and emotive manner popular among young African Americans may be interpreted as combative or argumentative by unfamiliar listeners. Fear may also contribute to over-referral. Teachers, who are prone to accepting stereotypes of adolescent African American males as threatening or dangerous, may overreact to relatively minor threats to authority, especially if their anxiety is paired with a misunderstanding of cultural norms of social interaction. (Skiba, Michael, Nardo & Peterson, 2000, p. 17)*

One reason for this disparity appears to be the lack of appropriate teacher training for novice and veteran teachers regarding the behaviors exhibited by students of color. Even though training has been provided, it often fails to focus on creating an understanding of the distinctions of these different cultures. Thus, while teachers are told to be culturally aware and understand the background of their students, instead they need to learn techniques to interpret situations and execute suitable actions. While the population of the country reflects differing cultures, the education system has failed to address the changes in the demographics of today's classrooms.

An additional implication of the study (Skiba, et al, 2000) related to the realization that school climate played a large role in the discipline referral system. "In this context, reducing the disciplinary gap between Black and White students may require attention to broad-scale systemic reform, whose goal is to equalize educational opportunity for all students" (Skiba, et al, 2000, p. 18).

Skiba, Michael, Nardo and Peterson (2000) noted that in schools with similar demographics, institutions with programs focusing on improving school climate and mentoring students saw a lower number of referrals and suspensions as compared to schools with authoritarian systems of discipline. This finding appeared to conclude that positive reinforcement of the culture, ethnicities and social backgrounds of students being supported through focused systems resulted in a more positive and healthy effect on the students' behavior, rather than a punitive discipline system. Further, results also noted a reduction in drop out rates and an increase in academic success (Skiba, et al, 2000).

Special Education Placement

As noted with discipline practices in educational institutions, a disparity exists in the number of students of color referred for special education placement. Oakes (2005) pointed out that poor and minority students consistently score lower on standardized assessments as compared to Whites. She postulated that this was due to the inherent unfairness of the placement tests themselves.

This result assumes special significance when considering tests that attempt to measure innate abilities or what we sometimes call native intelligence. We could judge such tests as fair only if poor and minority youngsters are less capable than middle- and upper-middle-class Whites. Despite some claims of a small group of researchers about a relationship between race and IQ, we simply do not have evidence that such a relationship exists. What we can be quite sure of, in fact, is that the ability to learn is normally distributed among and within social groups. (Oakes, 2005, p. 11)

Therefore, if evidence supports the fact that the ability to learn is not unique to one ethnic or social group, then an additional conclusion to be drawn is that the tests fail to provide an accurate measurement of the abilities and achievement potential of all students. Placement tests, which are designed to measure innate abilities or native intelligence should, by definition, suggest that students tested be given an assessment unique to their cultural background. However, the current practice in the American educational system is not based on the culture of students of color and students living in poverty. These populations often have difficulty with the standard academic placement assessments. Based on the tests' results, different groups of students appear to possess 'innate abilities' or 'native intelligences' dissimilar to those possessed by the middle-class, White student.

In regard to the over-representation of students of color enrolled in special education, it is not necessarily the teaching approach nor the curriculum that needs the most scrutiny and change. Rather, it is the way in which students' learning and abilities are measured. Renovating the testing structure appears necessary to create a system, which fairly measures the abilities of every student. If the results of years of research across racial and social barriers regarding the ability to learn are to be implemented, then the proportionality of students of color served by special education should closely mirror the racial and social make-up of the educational institutions serving them.

Academic Achievement

One of the goals of the *No Child Left Behind Act of 2001* (NCLB) was to close the achievement gap existing between affluent and poor children and between European American (White) students and students of color; thereby, leading to a system where all students could equally achieve success. Yet, when school districts disaggregate testing and achievement data, the widespread testing results continue to be higher levels of achievement for the affluent and the European American, or White, students and varying rates of achievement for poor and students of color (National Assessment of Educational Progress [NAEP], 2011). These discrepancies in achievement appear to be due to the lack of alignment between the objectives taught and those tested. Further, the objectives taught and tested fail to be relevant to the lives and experiences of students of color and those living in poverty. Knaus (2009) noted that students of color and those representing lower socio-economic backgrounds tend to be less likely to continue to attend a school in which they do not feel valued or relevant especially when they lack support at home (Tanner, 2007); thereby, resulting in low attendance and higher drop out rates for these under-served students.

Educators, who promote Critical Race Theory (CRT), advocate for the application of CRT. To combat the racism inherent in the current educational system, changes must begin to take place at the classroom level in local school districts. It is the teachers, who work with students of color and students representing the lower socio-economic groups daily, who have the ability to affect change in these areas (Tanner, 2007).

What makes Critical Race Theory applied is the focus on expression of voice and narrative by students, who are intentionally silenced by the everyday practices of schooling in the U. S. Applied CRT therefore, challenges the status quo of mainstream U. S. colonial-based, schooling by creating the structures through which student voice, particularly the voice of students of color, can develop, thrive, and express in culturally affirming and relevant ways. Applied CRT argues that what educators need to know about why schooling fails can be found in listening to students. (Knaus, 2009, p. 142)

It logically follows that when students are taught in a relevant, meaningful way, in which they are able to express their processing and learning in authentic ways, the retention of the required material will be greater (Tanner, 2007). But it is not only the teaching that must change, it is also the assessment materials being taught. As is evident in the misalignment of special education placement testing, if the test does not provide an accurate account of the child's ability, then the test is flawed.

Implications for Education

Although CRT posits that the current educational system was created by and continues to put a high priority on the beliefs of the White majority, it does not state that all Whites are racist nor that it is the fault of the current White majority that under-served students continue to fail within the present educational system. Rather, the more obvious fact is that the system itself is outdated and faulty. However, based on CRT, the responsibility for change is that of all educators, those representing both minority and majority ethnicities. The difficulty of change for many educators is to understand the problem without becoming emotionally attached to their own roles within the problem and its solution.

As critical race theorists point out, racism is not an individual pathology, rather it is a systemic structural problem that is constructed and maintained by the collective acts of many individuals, but which is larger and far more powerful than any individual. (Vaught & Castagno, 2008, p. 101)

So the goal of CRT is to accurately view and evaluate the current system and its support, or lack thereof, and to view and evaluate the education and advancement of all students, not just those who fall into the majority or affluent categories.

Summary of Findings

• CRT is used to provide explanation for the achievement gap between students of color, those living in poverty and their European American, or White, majority counterparts.

• CRT posits that innate racism exists within the American educational and legal systems.

• CRT states that the problematic systems in America are products of a time when the majority represented White, male, property owners, who controlled the legal and educational systems.

• CRT supports the principle that although much of the racial makeup and leadership of these systems have changed, their basic structures and tenets have not; thus leading to a contradiction, which result in low performance of under-served populations.

• CRT theorists, who advocate real change, encourage collaborative change within these systems to create fair practices, while incorporating the individual experiences of all cultural groups.

• CRT advocates the position that changing the educational system to incorporate the shared and individual experiences of under-served groups will results in a more balanced representation of these groups within programs, such as special education and gifted and talented education as well as a change in discipline practices.

• CRT notes that change in the American education system may result in success for all students regardless of racial or socio-economic background, will require fundamental transformation in the organization and structures upon which the educational system is built. Further, assumptions must change.

CASE STUDY 1
Critical Race Theory

Ms. Ramirez, a fourth year teacher at Allendar Middle School, decided to try a new approach with her English Language Arts class this year. Over the past three school years, she had found it difficult to connect with many of her students. The school population is 47% African American, 30% Hispanic, 15% East Asian, and the remainder a mixture of Caucasian, Pacific Islander, African, and Native American. The curriculum that she was required to cover focused on preparing the students for standardized testing during the spring semester. The standards to be addressed included reading skills and a repetition of grammar concepts. However, when using the methods promoted by the state and the school district, her African American and Hispanic students failed to be successful on these tests. Ms. Ramirez also noticed that she was having increasing discipline problems with her African American students. When analyzing her referral rates, she noticed that she had referred African American students to the office four times more often than any other racial group.

Determined to change the climate of her classroom, Ms. Ramirez spent a great deal of time at the beginning of the year learning about the personalities and interests of her students. She allowed the students to keep a journal and share their thoughts with their peers. She frequently responded to their writings and validated their feelings. It was through this practice that she was able to get a glimpse of the inner worlds of many of her struggling students. Using this growing collection of information, Ms. Ramirez began creating assignments and grammar exercises that directly related to the experiences and interests of her students. Having brought relevance to the material and shown genuine interest in her students' worlds, Ms. Ramirez began to see a marked improvement in their test results. Additionally, the discipline problems decreased rapidly in her class. When students were asked how the class was different, they frequently responded: "Ms. Ramirez teaches us about stuff that matters to us. This class isn't about English; it's about my story and telling it."

Questions for Reflection

1. How do the curriculum adjustments made by Ms. Ramirez demonstrate an understanding of Critical Race Theory?

2. According to CRT, what accounts for the change in student success rate in Ms. Ramirez's class?

3. What explains the improvement in behavior for the students in Ms. Ramirez's class?

4. What challenges does Ms. Ramirez face since she has diverted instruction from the district and state curriculum?

5. How can Ms. Ramirez help change the overall climate of her school?

References

Gordon, R., Piana, L. D., & Keleher, T. (2000). *Facing the consequences: An examination of racial discrimination in U.S. public schools.* (ERASE Initiative Reports-Descriptive 141). Retrieved from ERASE Initiative Applied Research Center website: http://www.arc.org.

Knaus, C. (2009) Shut up and listen: Applied critical race theory in the classroom. *Race Ethnicity and Education, 12(2)*, 133–154.

National Assessment of Educational Progress (2011). *Reading achievement gaps.*[Data file]. Retrieved from http://nces.ed.gov/programs/coe/indicator_rgp.asp.

U. S. Department of Education. No Child Left Behind Act (2001). *Title I - Improving the academic achievement of the disadvantaged.* Retrieved from http://www2.ed.gov/policy/elsec/leg/esea02/pg1.html.

Oakes, J. (2005) *Keeping track: How schools structure inequality* (2nd ed.). New Haven: Yale University Press.

Powers, J. (2007) The relevance of critical race theory to educational theory and practice. *Journal of Philosophy of Education, 41(1)*, 151-166.

Skiba, R., Michael, R., Nardo, A., & Peterson, R. (2000). *The color of discipline: Sources of racial and gender disproportionality in school punishment.* Bloomington: Indiana University.

Tanner, T. (2007). Embracing the Challenge: Closing the achievement gap through culturally responsive educators. *Journal of the Alliance of Black School Educators, 6(1)* 29-36.

Vaught, S., & Castagno, A. (2008) "I don't think I'm a racist": Critical Race Theory, teacher attitudes, and structural racism. *Race Ethnicity and Education. 11(2)*, 95–113.

CHAPTER 4
Pygmalion Effect:
The Concept of the Self-Fulfilling Prophecy

Pygmalion is the story of the rich and powerful king of Cyprus, who carved a beautiful statue of stone. The statue was so lovely that he fell in love with it. The goddess Aphrodite felt pity on Pygmalion and turned the statue into a living woman (Hamilton, 1942). George Bernard Shaw (1916) later adapted the story to modern times in his play entitled, Pygmalion. In the story, a linguistics professor is determined to turn a poor young flower seller into a beautiful woman of high society (Shaw, 1916). The message seemed to be, if you have high enough expectations, those expectations can be realized.

Theoretical Framework

The Pygmalion Effect, or the idea of the self-fulfilling prophecy, has its modern origins in a study conducted by Robert Rosenthal in 1968 (Rosenthal & Jacobson, 1968). The study gave a group of elementary school students an IQ test at the beginning of the school year. After the test, the teachers were told that a specific group of students were predicted to excel during that school year. Eight months later, the students were tested again using the same assessment. The results showed that the group of students predicted to perform at a higher level, fulfilled that prediction. Of the implications resulting from the study, three will be explored:

• Based on many factors, teachers develop expectations for students' future achievements.

- The teacher's and students' actions are directly influenced by pre-conceived notions of achievement.

- A student's self-image and sense of worth are directly impacted by the results of these expectations and subsequent actions.

Teacher Expectations

When a new group of students enters the classroom for the first time, teachers are hard pressed not to make judgments about the individual students according to immediate first impression observations. Additionally, during the first two weeks of school, both the teacher and the student are learning about each other

> A teacher's view of a student or group of students can be so powerful, his or her mind will seek to find the evidence necessary to support that view.

through observation and behavior patterns. During this time period the self-fulfilling prophecy, or Pygmalion effect, may come into realization.

The powerful influence of expectations of others on behavior and self-esteem has been dubbed the Pygmalion effect. A common expression illustrating the power of the Pygmalion effect goes like this:
> *I am not what I think I am.*
> *I am not what you think I am.*
> *I am what I think you think I am.*

Pygmalion-self is our perception of what we believe other people think of us. Thus, Pygmalion-self is precisely what the expression above exclaims: 'I am what I think you think I am'. (Page & Page, 2003, p. 39)

Students perceive and interpret the meanings of their teacher's behavior. This interpretation influences the expectations they set for themselves; thereby, affecting academic performance. Therefore, the Pygmalion effect appears to be influenced not only by the actions of the present teacher, but also the perceptions of former teachers and people of influence, who have impacted the student's life.

> *The Pygmalion effect, as we know it today, suggests that people give back to others the behavior they sense others expect of them. An athlete executes a play in a superior way because the coach expects it of him or her; a student excels in the classroom because his or her teacher communicates the belief and expectation that the student is capable of performing that way. (Harris & Hartman, 2002, p. 192)*

Unfortunately, the idea of the self-fulfilling prophecy does not always work in positive ways. In Rosenthal's study, it was determined that the students in the control group, those without higher expectations, were in some cases treated in a negative way when they did exceed expectations. Additionally, students perceived by their teachers as possessing lower abilities, often exhibited inappropriate behavior in the classroom.

Teacher/Student Actions

The largest part of the Pygmalion Effect is resulting behaviors from the perceptions of the teacher, the student, and those around them.

> *The Pygmalion Effect, on the other hand, is the observed effect whereby people come to behave in ways that correspond to others' expectations concerning them. The Pygmalion effect is similar, functionally, to the concept of self-fulfilling prophecy/prediction, that is, things turn out just as one expected or prophesied that they would, not necessarily because of one's prescience but because one behaved in a manner that optimized those very outcomes. (Roeckelein, 2006, p. 504)*

Teachers' behaviors send messages influencing ways students view themselves as potential achievers or students at risk of failure. These behaviors are subconscious; many times hard to pin point; and unseen until the damage has already been done.

The literature suggests that self-fulfilling prophecies are often medi-ated by expectancy-revealing perceiver's expressive behaviors, e.g. behaviors that suggest to a target how a perceiver feels about him or her. Such expressions may be communicated both nonverbally and verbally, either intentionally or not. Importantly, expectancies influence such expressive behaviors, and these behaviors influence the actions of others. (Neuberg, Judice, Virdin, & Carrillo, 1993, p. 410)

Actions as simple as how frequently a teacher calls on a student, the amount of parental contact and the extent of basic conversation be-tween the teacher and student, influence the student's perceptions of the teacher's expectations. This is especially true of interactions between teachers and perceived low achievers. In these interactions, teachers often demonstrate behaviors such as insincere praise, less frequent and infor-mative feedback, paying less attention to the student, making less contact with the student and using less of the student's ideas.

The first factor, climate, refers to the warmer socio-emotional cli-mate that teachers tend to create for high-expectancy students, a warmth that can be communicated both verbally and non verbally. The input factor refers to the tendency for teachers to teach more material to their 'special' students. The output factor refers to the tendency for teachers to give their 'special' students greater oppor-tunities for responding. Finally, the feedback factor refers to the tendency for teachers to give more differentiated feedback to their 'special,' high-expectancy students. By differentiated, we mean that the feedback will be contingent on the correctness or incorrectness of the student's response and that the content of the feedback will tend to be directly related to what the student has said. (Rosenthal, 2002, p. 33)

Student Achievement

Stereotyping and the other effects of cultural-ecology can magnify the Pygmalion Effect in students. When there is a pre-conceived cultural perception of a group, as being inferior, whether that perception comes from within the culture itself, or is projected by the educational system, students can enter the system with a Pygmalion-self that is ill equipped to break down those stereotypes. Compound this with a system stuck in the self-fulfilling prophecy cycle of perceiving students as low performers, many students have little hope of achieving excellence (Kuklinski & Weinstein, 2001). Subsequent research suggested that Pygmalion Effects resulted in changes to student's expectations. When teachers perceived that students would do well, the students adopted a similar set of elevated expectations, resulting in increased achievement (Kuklinski & Weinstein, 2001).

The variations in teacher's expectations may contribute to the differential success rates of majority students, students of color and those living in poverty. Teachers hold the highest expectations for Asian American students and the lowest expectations for Hispanic American and African American students (Tenenbaum & Ruck, 2007) Student performance mirrors these expectations (Park & Clarke-Stewart, 2011).

Some students are more influenced than others, which may account for the fact that some of them excel under a different teacher. This could be a result of the teacher having higher expectations for the student, or higher expectations being given by family, friends, peers, or significant others.

Implications for Education

Teachers should believe that each child comes to school with limitless potential. The Pygmalion Effect can be a powerful tool for student achievement. It is often viewed as an underlying reason for student achievement or student failure. Further, teachers and administrators are often unaware of its existence in their classrooms and campuses. But in

reality, the prejudices and biases of teachers and administrators often sig-
nificantly affect students' achievement more so than other practices.

> *During the Civil Rights Era of the mid-20th century, school desegre-*
> *gation activists realized that simply changing the social organiza-*
> *tion of schools and the curriculum would have little effect on the*
> *achievement of students of color and working-class poor students*
> *unless a concomitant change occurred in the minds of school per-*
> *sonnel and school partners. Moreover, activities pointed out that*
> *disadvantaged children did not possess problems or have some*
> *deficit that needed remediation, but that changing the attitude of*
> *school personnel and school partners toward disadvantaged chil-*
> *dren would be more effective. (Schramm-Pate, 2010, p. 700)*

According to Banks (2002), "through an empowering school
culture and social structure, grouping and labeling practices, disproportionality in achievement and the interaction between faculty and students
across ethnic and racial lines are among the components of school culture" (Banks, 2002, p. 14). He feels that these must be examined to create
a school culture that empowers students representing diverse racial, ethnic and cultural groups. Through reflection, schools can evaluate whether
or not faculty members have biases and prejudices, which would affect
how they view students. Then more efficient training focusing on the
tenets of multicultural education can be scheduled and follow-up sessions
and observations could determine whether or not change is being made.

> *By becoming aware of the major factors that influence teachers'*
> *perceptions of and actions toward students, you may be able to re-*
> *duce subjectivity to a minimum, particularly with students whose*
> *cultural backgrounds are very different from your own. (Snowman,*
> *McCown, and Biehler, 2009, p. 158)*

Gathering data and other information helps a teacher establish a
student's baseline information. However, using that information to label
a student negatively affects the student's self-concept and future poten-

tial. Through the Pygmalion Effect, teachers can impact whether or not a student is academically successful and reaching his or her full potential. Teachers who possess an affirmative outlook regarding their students' abilities positively affect their students' futures (Rosenthal & Jacobson, 1968).

CASE STUDY 1
Pygmalion Effect

Monica was a 5th grader beginning the year at a new school. Over the summer, her parents had moved to a new suburb on the other side of town and everything was different for her. As a quiet girl, she always had friends and was well liked, but typically struggled with her academics. In her old school, she had recently been exited from the special education program and was being tracked and supported through 504 modifications.

Monica's new teacher, Mrs. Stafford, was a conscientious, veteran teacher, who liked to learn a little about her students before she met them each year. The school had already called Monica's previous school to have her records transferred. Mrs. Stafford reviewed Monica's records in the registrar's office. Upon looking at Monica's academic file, she was pleased to discover that Monica had tested above her grade level in both reading comprehension and listening skills. Mrs. Stafford used this information to place Monica in an advanced reading group immediately when the year began.

As the year progressed, Monica struggled with her studies, but never complained about the workload. She had never been in an advanced reading group, but she was happy that her teacher apparently thought she was very smart. Her parents, who both worked outside the home, were oftentimes too busy to give her extra assistance. Monica made sure to ask questions in class when she was confused. She didn't want to disappoint Mrs. Stafford by failing any of her assignments.

At the end of the year, the students took the state assessment test, which included measuring reading comprehension and listening skills. The results revealed that Monica had registered in reading and listening at one grade level above normal. These results were confusing to Mrs. Stafford. She felt that surely with all of the work Monica had done, she should have made more gains. Instead it appeared that she had made no gains at all. Mrs. Stafford decided to research the situation and found that the wrong records had been sent from Monica's previous school. In reality, Monica had begun the year reading and listening two grade levels below her current level. Mrs. Stafford was astounded that she had not realized the discrepancy during the school year. She excitedly told Monica's parents about her gains.

Questions for Reflection

1. How is Monica's story an example of the Pygmalion Effect?

2. In this case, how did the self-fulfilling prophecy have positive results?

3. How could this situation have had a negative effect on Monica?

4. How can Mrs. Stafford use this experience to reflect and adjust her actions for the future?

5. Describe Monica's Pygmalion-self in this situation.

CASE STUDY 2
Pygmalion Effect

Jared began his senior year at Parkview High School. He is a very popular young man, handsome, tall, and athletic. He is one of those people that other people gravitate toward.

Mr. Scott, the high school's economics teacher, has been teaching at Parkview for 25 years. All students have to take economics from him; there is no other alternative. Mr. Scott takes pride in his focus on academics and what he thinks is his perfect judge of character and ability in his students.

The moment Jared enters his classroom, Mr. Scott anticipates problems. Jared wears the self-confident smile of a young man, who is used to being accommodated. He carries a football in one hand, his iPhone in the other, and is flanked by two cheerleaders.

"Hey, there Scotty!" Jared calls to Mr. Scott.

"I will be addressed as Mr. Scott or sir, young man." Mr. Scott replies.

"Whoa, no problemo… " Jared replies. "Wow, he's a tough one isn't he?" he continues under his breath. The girls around him giggle.

Mr. Scott immediately thinks, "Great, another stupid jock, who thinks he'll get a good grade just because the football team needs him to play." Mr. Scott groans inwardly at the prospect of a long semester. He has had students like Jared before and they all end up being the same: annoying, not serious, disruptive and cocky. Mr. Scott has had it with the sense of entitlement that the athletes seem to have on this campus.

As the semester continues, Mr. Scott and Jared constantly butt heads. Jared rarely turns in homework, barely passes his tests and is disruptive whenever the opportunity presents itself. Mr. Scott has sent frequent emails to Jared's coaches, but sees no real improvement.

In the teacher's lounge one day, Mr. Scott decides to ask his colleagues about Jared.

"Do any of you have Jared Williams in your classes?"

"Oh yes, he is one of my favorite students!" the art teacher replies. "He is so polite and courteous. Such a gentlemen!"

"I have Jared in AP Calculus." Mr. Carr states. "He is indispensable as a tutor for the other struggling students."

"Jared is in my AP English class." Mrs. Stedman pipes in. "Such a well rounded young man. I wish all of our athletes were like him!"

Mr. Scott is confused by the feedback he has just received. They couldn't possibly be describing the same student that has been a thorn in his side for three-quarters of a semester already. He decides it is time for a conference with Jared and his parents. He schedules one for the very next day.

"Mr. and Mrs. Williams, thank you so much for meeting with me today." Mr. Scott began.

"We were pleased to hear from you." Mr. Williams replied. "Jared's other teachers have kept in close contact. We noticed that he was not excelling in your class and knew there must be some explanation."

Mr. Scott proceeded to explain his experiences with Jared over the course of the semester. He explained the encounters they had in class and the contact he had established with Jared's coaches. He also showed samples of Jared's work and explained his low grade.

"Jared, what do you have to say about all of this?" Mr. Williams inquired of his son.

"Well, sir, Mr. Scott had already made up his mind about me when I entered the class on the first day. He did not show me respect so I repaid the favor."

"Son, we have taught you better than that. You need to apologize to Mr. Scott."

"I know. I'm sorry, Mr. Scott. But let me say this, it is unfair to judge someone before you even know them. Just because I look like every other stupid entitled jock that has entered your room, does not mean I am the same."

Questions for Reflection

1. What assumptions did Mr. Scott make about Jared when he first met him?

2. What role did Mr. Scott play in the behavior and academic outcome of the athletes in his class?

3. How and why did Jared 'live up' to those expectations?

4. How could Mr. Scott have solved his problem earlier in the school year?

5. How did this experience negatively impact Jared?

6. Do you think Mr. Scott realized that he was participating in the Pygmalion Effect?

7. How should he adjust his procedures and/or prejudices to prevent this situation from happening in the future?

REFERENCES

Banks, J. A. (2002). *An introduction to multicultural behavior*. Boston: Allyn & Bacon.

Hamilton, E. (1942). *Mythology*. New York: Little, Brown, and Company.

Harris, O. J., & Hartman, S. J. (2002). *Organizational behavior.* Binghamton: Haworth Press, Inc.

Neuberg, S. L., Judice, T. N., Virdin, L. M., & Carrillo, M. A. (1993). Perceiver self-presentational goals as moderators of expectancy influences: Ingratiation and the confirmation of negative expectancies. *Journal of Personality and Social Psychology, 64(3),* 409-420.

Page, R. M., & Page, T. S. (2003) *Fostering emotional well-being in the class room*. Burlington: Jones & Bartlett Publishers.

Roeckelein, J. E. (2006.) *Elsevier's dictionary of psychological theories*. San Diego: Elsevier, Inc.

Rosenthal, R., and Jacobson, L. (1968). *Pygmalion in the classroom: Teacher expectation and pupils' intellectual development*. New York: Rinehart & Winston.

Rosenthal, R. (2002) The Pygmalion effect and its mediating mechanisms. In J. M. Aronson (Ed.), *Improving academic achievement: Impact of psychological factors on education.* (pp. 25-36). San Diego: Academic Press.

Shaw, G. B. (1913). *Pygmalion*. London: Penguin Classics.

Snowman, J., McCown, R. P., & Biehler, R. (2009) *Psychology applied to teaching*. Boston: Houghton Mifflin Company.

Tenenbaum, H. & Ruck, M. (2007) Are teachers' expectations different for racial Minorities than for European American students? A Meta-Analysis. *Journal of Educational Psychology, 99,* 253-73.

CHAPTER 5
Locus of Control Theory

Picture this conversation occurring during the weekly professional learning community meeting:

Curriculum Supervisor: Take a moment to evaluate why your students are not experiencing the desired outcome. What do you think is the reason behind the lack of academic achievement?

Teacher A: Well, ever since they built those apartments across the street, our scores have dropped like a boulder in the ocean.

Teacher B: We don't get enough planning time and resources. Plus, our students don't really try or study at all. I'm doing all that I can. It's not my fault they can't learn.

Teacher C: I think I need to find a way to quickly assess the students and check for understanding. I have a high mobility rate in my classroom so it's important to make sure that the new students are on the same page as the rest of the students before we move forward. Maybe doing a better job of tracking their progress and adjusting my teaching to fit what is needed... That's what I want to try.

Teacher D: I've been assessing, but that doesn't seem to be helping. I have a hard time finding time to analyze the data I get from the assessments.

Theoretical Framework

The teachers above represent different beliefs about how much control they personally have in determining the academic success of their students. This chapter will address the Locus of Control (LOC) theory. This theory explains where individuals conceptually place responsibility, choice, and control for events in their lives.

> *People with an internal Locus of Control (LOC) orientation tend to perceive their actions as influencing the outcomes they experience, whereas people with an external LOC orientation tend to perceive their actions as having little or no influence on the outcomes they experience. Instead, they perceive outside forces, such as powerful others, luck, or chance, as the influencing factor. (Shogren, Boviard, Palmer, & Wehmeyer, 2010, p. 81)*

The LOC theory distinguishes between two common approaches; control is placed either internally or externally to the person. Individuals with an *internal* locus of control (internals) view the events in their life as a product of their own actions (Rotter, 1990). These individuals are more likely to take responsibility for their actions and tend to learn from mistakes and change their course to avoid them in the future. Internals also feel strongly that they have the ability to control their environment to achieve the results they desire.

Conversely, individuals with an *external* locus of control (externals) view events in their life as controlled by external factors (Rotter, 1990). These individuals often experience failure more often than success and feel strongly that there is nothing they can do to change their circumstances. Externals frequently see their lives as controlled by luck or fate and have difficulty taking responsibility for their successes or failures. The idea of locus of control can affect both students and teachers alike, both with major consequences.

Student Achievement

Education is, and of course should be, focused on student achievement. Understanding the LOC theory and its affect on student achievement will help in bridging the gap existing between low performing and high performing students. "For example, it was observed that students whose orientation was internal were characterized [as] higher achievers in educational expectations and aspirations than students whose orientation was external [which] marked the low academic achievement among students" (Uguak, Elias, Uli & Suandi, 2009, p. 126).

Students who take responsibility for their actions or attempt to understand the source for their successes and failures, are more likely to be academically successful because they seek to learn from their experiences. This act demonstrates ownership and the desire to control the circumstances of their environment. This frame of mind can be sharply contrasted with that of an external.

[Many] failure-oriented individuals contributed outcomes to be caused by external factors; namely, the difficulty level of the tasks or bad luck. Those failure-oriented persons were strongly influenced by prior negative expectancies; they usually had low success expectancy and set themselves unrealistic goals, which were either too high or too low. (Uguak, Elias, Uli & Suandi, 2009, p. 121)

The act of setting realistic goals can help a student in transforming from an external into an internal. Although other factors contribute to an individual's view of the world, in terms of academic achievement, setting and achieving realistic academic goals and then understanding the reasons behind the success or failure assists to transform them into more successful students (Galbraith & Alexander, 2005). During this instance, the teacher can be a powerful influence in a student's life.

As some students clearly took blame for their dismal failures, it could result in debilitating losses in motivation, adjustment, atti-

tude, self-efficacy, attribution, locus of control, and so on. To coun-
teract those "natural" attribution tendencies, educators should
encourage students to explore the causes of their academic achieve-
ment dissatisfaction, while guiding them toward achievement pro-
moting conclusions about causality. (Uguak, Elias, Uli & Suandi,
2009, p. 127)

Teacher Behavior

Teacher behavior can describe the behavior of the teacher as an individual and the behavior the teacher needs to exhibit in order to adjust and encourage the actions of their students. The LOC of the individual, employed as a teacher, will influence the success of that individual as a teacher of students. Teachers, who possess an internal LOC, continually evaluate their performance based on what they see as factors they can control. These individuals are eager to seek out solutions to address low performance and are reflective of their students' achievement (Ignat & Clipa, 2010). Because of their internal LOC, they are more likely to be successful and lead their students to success.

If a teacher feels that he or she has no control over the outcome of what they teach, they are demonstrating an external LOC. These are the teachers who blame everyone else for the performance of their students. They are less likely to take responsibility for their performance and are not usually considered to be self-reflective. Teachers who experience an external LOC are likely to experience less success.

Teachers who desire to help their students gain control over their academic performance can begin by taking ownership of the outcomes produced in their classroom. Demonstrating and modeling the behavior of reflecting on the results of their work and learning how to increase their knowledge teaches them to possess an internal LOC. By evaluating the reasons behind their success or failure, their LOC moves toward the internal.

If children can see their own role in the educational process as significant they may be encouraged to persevere in the face of difficulty... Children who are encouraged to plan, carry out and then reflect on their own work ('Plan-Do-Review' in the Interactivist's terminology) 'may increase their self-management skills and internality of locus of control.' (Galbraith & Alexander, 2005, p. 29)

Helping students understand techniques they can use will allow them to take control of their environment and influence what occurs in their lives. This action will not only lead to increased self-confidence, but also increased academic success. It is this aspect of practical education that can most effectively combat the learned helplessness occurring among students, who face difficult life situations (Galbraith & Alexander, 2005). Teachers who themselves are individuals with an internal locus of control, will find it easier to impart that world-view to their students.

Summary of Locus of Control Theory

Internals	Externals
• work for achievement • tolerate delay in rewards • plan for long-term goals	• more likely to lower their goals
• resist coercion or intimidation	• possess a higher outer-directedness • are more vulnerable to coercion
• tolerate ambiguous situations • may be less prone to depression • more prone to feelings of guilt	• tend to feel they have less control over their fate • are prone to learned helplessness
• less willing to take risks • less willing to work on self-improvement and better themselves	• tend to be more stressed • are prone to clinical depression
• prefer games based on skill	• prefer games based on chance or luck

CASE STUDY 1
Locus of Control Theory

Anastasia walks into the room and slams her books on the desk. "Man! Why do these things always happen to me?" she yells to no one in particular.

"What is the problem?" asks Mrs. Channing. "What's got you so upset?"

"Oh, I got an F on my math test. Ms. Graves hates me."

"Why do you think that?"

"Because I always fail my math tests. AND, she refuses to help me." Anastasia sulks.

"Have you asked her for help?" Mrs. Channing inquires.

"No, but she wouldn't help me anyway."

"Do you ask questions in small group time? Does Ms. Graves check for understanding in class?"

"I shouldn't have to ask questions. That's what stupid people have to do. I just didn't get the math gene, I guess."

"Anastasia, you can't just expect to know something like math without putting any effort into it. You have to ask questions. Do the students who ask questions in class, get better grades on their assignments?"

"Yes, but they are just smarter than me" replies Anastasia.

"No, they know that if they don't understand how to work the problems, they have to ask or they won't learn. It has nothing to do with whether or not you have a natural aptitude for math. Instead, it has to do with asking questions when you don't understand, answering Ms. Graves questions, whether you try, and your work on the subjects that are difficult for you. Now, show me your test, let's look and see if we can't figure out what went wrong. Then we can come up with a plan to help you for the next test."

"Alright, but I don't see why you are bothering."

"I *bother* because I care and I know you can be in control of your academic success. You just have to adjust the way you are thinking about your learning."

Questions for Reflection

1. Does Anastasia have an internal or external locus of control? What evidence is given?

2. How does Mrs. Channing try to help Anastasia?

3. Imagine Anastasia in other situations around the school. How do you think she would react in a conflict situation? Why?

4. What steps can Mrs. Channing and Ms. Graves take to help Anastasia change her mindset and experience success?

CASE STUDY
Locus of Control Theory

Refer back to the PLC conversation at the beginning of this chapter.

1. What type of locus of control do teachers A, B, C, and D reflect?

2. How does their LOC impact their students? How might the academic success of their students be impacted if they were able to switch their locus of control?

REFERENCES

Galbraith, A., & Alexander, J. (2005). Literacy, self-esteem and locus of control. *Support for Learning, 20(1),* 28-34.

Ignat, A., & Clipa, O. (2010). The impact of self-efficacy and locus of control on the professional development of the teachers. *Bulletin: University Petrol-Gaze din Ploiesti, 64(1).* 180-185.

Rotter, J.B. (1990). Internal versus external control of reinforcement: A case history of a variable. *American Psychologist, 45,* 489-493.

Shogren, K., Boviard, J., Palmer, S., & Wehmeyer, M. (2010). Locus of control orientations in students with intellectual disability, learning disabilities, and no disabilities: A latent growth curve analysis. *Research and Practice for Persons with Severe Disabilities, 35(3),* 80-92.

Uguak, U., Elias, H., Uli, J., & Suandi, T. (2009). The influence of causal elements of locus of control on academic achievement satisfaction. *Journal of Instructional Psychology, 34(2),* 120-128.

CHAPTER 6
Deficit Theory

Theoretical Framework

[The] Cultural Deficiency Theory suggests that family structure, values, languages and traditions [of students of color or students living in poverty] are somehow less than those of the Euro-immigrants, while [their] imposed values and lifestyles have been positioned as models to be emulated. (Jackson & Solis, 1995, p. 114)

> Rationalization 1: Success in school is directly related to the genetic pathology of an individual or group.

The deficit theory is one of the most dangerous in terms of depriving students of a quality education. In deficit theory, the belief is that some students, due to factors beyond their control, simply do not have the tools necessary to thrive and succeed in their educational endeavors. When students are unsuccessful, the blame is first placed on their background, socio-economic status, racial heritage and family circumstances, rather than on factors which can be changed such as poor teaching, low expectations of the students, incorrect placement or lack of consistent structure.

Deficit theory finds its roots in the seventeenth century as Europeans moved onto the North American continent and began to exploit and gain dominance over the indigenous populations. These populations were viewed through eyes, which saw their unique characteristics as deficiencies when compared to the so-called 'civilized' Europeans. Instead of seeking to discover the strengths of the existing population, European immigrants sought to establish and maintain control over them. "To many individuals, inferiority was associated with biological differences, whereas to others, it was a result of non-whites lacking European culture and/or Christian religion" (Menchaca, 1997, p. 16).

Three hundred years later, the effects of this policy of exploitation and dominance are evident. Our educational system continues to cater to the majority population.

> Rationalization 2: Success in school is directly related to cultural backgrounds including ethnicity and economic status.

Minority populations are expected to change or comply in order to be successful in this system. Many times, when examining the achievement gap in education, a distinct set of characteristics defines the struggling learner, including socio-economic status, racial heritage, and family circumstances. When viewed through the lens of deficit theory, these characteristics are explained as reasons for students of color and those living in poverty to be unsuccessful. However, upon a more thoughtful and reflective investigation, many of these students are not being served in the same conditions as the students of the majority population due to unacknowledged prejudices.

That is, teachers operating under a Deficit Model Curriculum do not trust students' abilities to think critically and arrive at conclusions that approximate the right answer. The Deficit Model does not provide students with opportunities to think more critically, take risks, and problem solve without penalty. Curricula that do not facilitate critical thinking restrict learning and encourage deficit thinking. (Green, 2006, p. 25)

The rationalizations used by proponents of deficit theory, the impact that the theory has on education, and adjustments which can be made to better serve all students will be explored. Naturally, generalizations are made as a way of categorizing the information we acquire to make sense of it. "Humans are objectified by assigning them names or labels for their particular behaviors and characteristics, e.g., schizophrenic, blind, poor, girl" (Lindsey, Robins, & Terrell, 2009, p. 28).

Whether we have heard it blatantly used, or have simply seen it in action, it is hard to deny that genetic profiling happens daily in education. It is difficult to refrain from comparing students, who come from the same family or who belong to a particular ethnic group. A teacher might remember how difficult Alex was as a student and how the highest grade he managed to obtain was a C. Therefore, when his little brother, Joe, comes along, preconceived ideas about Joe's ability to achieve have been established.

Alternately, many believe that "all Asians are smart" or "all Blacks are loud." It is the gross generalization, which distracts from the recognition of the individual possessing a unique set of characteristics. When viewed through this rationalization, the student is already at a disadvantage before even setting foot into the classroom.

Science has taught us that certain physical characteristics share unique genetic markers. Great thinkers and writers such as Aristotle, Thomas Jefferson and Charles Darwin delivered their own theories and generalizations regarding the physical and intellectual abilities of individuals and groups (Valencia & Solorzano, 1997). Many of these theories have been embraced as fact. Due to these writings, people of color and those living in poverty have found themselves marginalized because of features and characteristics that are outside of the norm and therefore, they are considered lacking.

Deficit theorists would explain marginalization by stating that these groups have an inherent deficit in their genetic makeup. However, the research clearly states that no genetic connection exists between intellectual capacity and ethnic and/or genetic makeup.

> Rationalization 3: Our mind has a responsibility to find evidence to support our views. Deficit model teachers will continue to see what they believe and ignore that which contradicts their views.

The Cultural Deficit Theory states that some students do poorly in school because the linguistic, social, and cultural nature of the home environment does not prepare them for the work they will be required to do in school. (Lynch, 2011, p. 1)

Through this rationalization, the educational impact of the deficit theory is realized. In general, Deficit Theorists believe that the development of skills and experiences necessary to succeed in the western education system are directly related to culture and economic status. For example, if you are poor, you might be less likely to travel or to have books read to you as a child. This would then result in a lack of knowledge, experiences and exposure to global topics and concepts as well as a lack of literacy in the home. Because being able to read is a primary factor in academic success, students entering kindergarten with the ability to read already have experienced a greater advantage than other classmates, who have not experienced being read to or cannot recognize isolated alphabetic letters and their sounds. "Deficit theories assume that some children, because of genetic, cultural, or experiential differences, are inferior to other children; that is, they have a deficit" (Nieto, 2004, p. 3). However, this belief is directly related to the importance placed on these activities by different cultures and economic backgrounds. "[All] Children come to school with much knowledge. Many children, who do not succeed in schools, come with knowledge that is different from what educators expect" (Rozansky-Lloyd, 2005, p. 602).

The Deficit Theory relates with Critical Race Theory, previously addressed in this book, in that the current U. S. Education System was designed in the early twentieth century by the ruling elite in an attempt to 'civilize' the large number of immigrants migrating to America. Since that time, changes to the overall structure of the system have been limited. The present system fails to embrace differences and change. The Critical Race Theorist believes the differences of the populations of color in America have not been embraced, but rather forced into conformity. Being a member of a different race from the White, Anglo Saxon majority or having a limited amount of economic capital results in disadvantages for those people of color living in the United States. Deficit theory reflects an attempt to explain the lack of achievement by placing the blame on an unchangeable genetic or cultural characteristic. In doing so, opportunities to rise to the full potential of a large portion of the U. S. population are limited. Power-wielders believe and indicate that people of color should also believe, that success for them is unreachable. Through the use of the deficit theory, people of color have more obstacles to overcome simply due to their ethnicity and culture.

Implications for Education

As stated, the impact of this theory is critical in that it presupposes that students cannot achieve because of their culture, ethnicity, or economic status. If a teacher believes this theory, no actual teaching or evaluation of the child as an individual will occur. As Green (2006) stated, "The deficit model encourages a self-fulfilling prophecy that nontraditional students will fail, regardless of their talents, skills, and potential" (p. 25).

When teachers who believe in the deficit theory, view racial differences combined with economic disadvantages as representative of
students of color enrolled in urban school districts, a high percentage of
students of color are enlisted in special education programs, while a low
percentage of students of color are represented in gifted and advanced
placement programs. Furthermore, discipline for that student population
becomes an increasing problem. As part of the deficit theory, this situation is often explained as being part of their inherent 'deficit'; when in
reality, the educational system is failing to serve this student population
(Skiba, Michael, Nardo, & Peterson, 2000).

*When the habit of looking for intrinsic deficit intertwines with a
habit of interpreting cultural and racial differences as a deficit, the
deck is powerfully loaded against poor students of color. (Harry &
Klinger, 2007, p. 21)*

It is easier to lay blame for lack of achievement on the student
than for teachers and administrators to be reflective of their beliefs and
teaching practices. Using the deficit theory to explain the lack of achievement for students of color and those representing high poverty populations effectively takes the blame away from the teacher and paralyzes them
from taking control of the events in their classroom. Since the student's
performance is external to both the student's and teacher's control; then
it's not Johnny's fault. He can't help that he was born into that culture,
ethnic group or socio-economic status. Unfortunately, when teachers and
administrators pass the blame onto situations, which fail to be addressed,
the potential for the student to excel and learn is minimized.

So What Now?

As educators must realize, the achievement gap can no longer be explained
through the use of the Deficit Theory. The time has come for educators
and researchers to investigate the reasons that 'disadvantaged' populations fail to succeed. Indeed, labeling these groups as 'disadvantaged' is

possibly the first issue that should be addressed. Viewing all students in terms of the successful experiences they bring to the classroom, rather than the knowledge they lack based on predetermined conditions, will unite educators for achieving the common goal of serving all students with integrity and equality.

> *If applied similarly to curriculum, leadership, and hierarchical school systems, the guiding paradigm becomes an asset model that incorporates positive language and labels, is visionary and strategic, and most importantly, is student-centered. Moving from a deficit to an asset model affords under-served students academic opportunities that might otherwise be unavailable to them. (Green, 2006, p. 26)*

CASE STUDY 1
Deficit Theory

Jose Reyes was born in the United States. His parents achieved legal immigration status prior to his birth. The dominant language spoken at home is Spanish. His father owns his own tree pruning company and his mother is a bilingual aide with the school system. Jose has attended school in Tyler Independent School District since he was age four when he was enrolled in the Pre-K Bilingual Program.

Currently, Jose is in the eighth grade at Tyler Middle School. His past records show that he has had trouble with behavior. Teachers note that he becomes frustrated with content easily and they suspect he has difficulty reading. Although he was born in the United States, he is still enrolled in an English as a Second Language class five days a week.

In third grade, Jose met minimum standards on the math test, but did not meet those in reading. During his fourth grade year, he met the reading standards, but not those in math. His fifth grade year, he was successful on both the science test and math test, but failed to meet the minimum requirements for the reading standards.

His sporadic test scores have been a concern. He was evaluated for dyslexia in sixth grade and qualified for the dyslexia program. Cut backs in the number of staff positions have limited the services of the dyslexia department. Specialists for the middle school campuses have a dual assignment and now serve high school students as well. They spend most their time updating records. Occasionally, classroom teachers are provided with modifications and ideas to support dyslexic students.

Jose's eighth grade teachers are concerned about his readiness for the upcoming standardized tests. They complain that it is difficult for him to sit still and listen to the lectures. Further, he rarely turns in homework and prefers to spend time on the football field instead of studying. The counselor has contacted central office to inquire if they can speed up Jose's special education testing and placement in the program. She contends that he will not be successful without the support of special education.

Jose has been meeting with the counselor weekly to discuss his classroom behavior. His parents try to attend parent conferences, but they are often unable to attend during the workday. After school, he is responsible for his siblings until his mother returns home from an additional part time job.

Questions for Reflection

1. What assumptions is the school making in regards to Jose's language development?

2. How has deficit model thinking permeated the practices of his teachers?

3. What factors were over looked by the teachers and counselors?

4. What additional information is needed before Jose is recommended for special education testing?

5. What are the consequences of placing Jose in special education?

REFERENCES

Green, D. (2006). Historically under-served students: What we know, what we still need to know. *New Directions for Community Colleges, 135,* 21-28.

Harry, B., & Klinger, J. (2007). Discarding the deficit model. *Educational Leadership, 5,* 16-21.

Jackson, S., & Solis, J. (1995). The Mexican experience. In P. L. Falcon (Ed.)., *Beyond Comfort Zones in Multiculturalism: Confronting the Politic of Privilege* (pp. 114-115).Westport: Bergin and Garvey.

Lindsey, R. B., Robins, K. N., & Terrell, R. T. (2009). *Cultural Proficiency: A Manual for School Leaders.* Thousand Oaks: Corwin.

Lynch, M. (2011, October 27). Examining the impact of culture on academic performance. Retrieved July 30, 2012 from http://www.huffingtonpost.com/matthew-lynch-edd/education-culture_b_1034197.html.

Menchaca, M. (1997). Early racist discourses: The roots of deficit thinking. In R. Valencia (Ed.), *The Evolution of Deficit Thinking: Educational Thought and Practice.* (pp. 160-210). London, Washington, D.C.: Falmer Press.

Nieto, S. (2004). *Affirming Diversity: The Socio-political Context of Multicultural Education.* Boston: Pearson.

Rozansky-Lloyd, C. (2005). African Americans in Schools: Tiptoeing around racism. *The Western Journal of Black Studies, 29(3),* 595-604.

Skiba, R., Michael, R., Nardo, A., & Peterson, R. (2000). *The Color of Discipline: Sources of Racial and Gender Disproportionality in School Punishment.* Bloomington: Indiana University.

Valencia, R., & Solorzano, D. (1997). Contemporary Deficit Thinking. In R. Valencia (Ed.), *The Evolution of Deficit Thinking: Educational Thought and Practice.* (pp. 160-210). London, Washington, D.C.: Falmer Press.

CHAPTER 7
Learning Styles Theory

Theoretical Framework

Throughout the years, multiple attempts have made to define learning styles. From the Multiple Intelligences Theory researched by Howard Gardner (1983) to the learning styles theories of David Kolb (1983), each proposed to explain the ways students learn. Understanding how students learn provides educators additional tools with which they could effectively teach different learners. In this chapter, the research of Pat Guild and Stephen Garger (1985) will be examined. Garger and Guild (1985) summarized the characteristics of field independent and field dependent learners and researched the connection between culture and learning styles and the effect these two factors have in effectively educating children.

Understanding a student's learning style and culture are essential in being able to effectively teach the student and in turn, for the student to learn. "[K]nowing each student, especially his or her culture, is essential preparation for facilitating, structuring, and validating successful learning for all students" (Guild, 1994, p. 16). "Many authors acknowledge the cultural conflict between the typical educational experiences in schools and some students and the typical learning experiences in schools. When a [student] is socialized in their homes differently from the school expectations and patterns, the [student] needs to make a difficult daily adjustment to the culture of the school and his or her teachers" (Guild, 1994, p. 19).

As we try to accommodate students' cultural and learning differences, it is most important to deeply value each person's individuality. If we believe that people do learn - and have the right to learn - in a variety of ways, then we will see learning styles as a comprehensive approach guiding all educational decisions and practices. (Guild, 1994, p. 21)

Field Dependent/Independent Learning

Field-dependent and Independent learning styles describe the different ways that people observe their environment and process information to be able to organize, interpret and use that information in their lives. Field dependence/independence are measured along a continuum, ranging from individuals, who are extremely field dependent (FD), to those who are extremely field independent (FI). FD students find it difficult to separate incoming information from the context in which it is received. They look at things in a global way and are more likely to be influenced by external clues as a way of interpreting the information they receive. FD students are also classified as global learners.

Students who are field independent are able to separate essential information from the context in which it is presented. They are much more sequential and they tend to be more selective about the information they accept; therefore, they are internally influenced. FI students can also be considered analytic learners (Guisande, Paramo, Tinajero & Almeida, 2007). Understanding the different ways that these two types of learners gain and process information, will allow educators to adjust their teaching to effectively reach each type of learner.

[Studies have] indicated that field dependence/field independence is unrelated to intelligence, but a difference in cognitive style can be a major factor in learning; the field-dependent person is likely to require more explicit guidance or external organizing structures

than the field-independent person. (Ku & Soulier, 2009, p. 654)

A field-dependent person has difficulty finding a geometric shape that is embedded or 'hidden' in a background with similar (but not identical) lines and shapes. The conflicting patterns distract the person from identifying the given figure. A person who is field-independent can readily identify the geometric shape, regardless of the background in which it is set. ("Cognitive Style", 2012)

The following table depicts the various characteristics of learning styles. It is important to also point out that this description of learning styles does not exclude the findings of other researchers, such as Gardner (1983) and Kolb (1983). Students can be kinesthetic learners and also be field-dependent or independent. Teachers, trained to fully understand all of the learning styles theories, can combine those theories learned and create a positive, effective learning experience for all students.

Learning Styles of FD and FI Students

Field-Dependent/Global	Field-Independent/Analytic
Perceives globally Looks at the whole, then the parts	Perceives analytically Looks at the parts, and decides how they fit into the whole
Experiences in a global fashion Adheres to structures as given	Experiences in an articulate fashion Imposes structures of restrictions
Makes broad general distinctions among concepts Sees relationships	Makes specific concept distinctions, little overlap
Social orientation	Impersonal orientation
Learns material best through social interaction	Learns social material only as an intentional task
Attends best when material is relevant to own experiences	Interested in new concepts for their own sake
Requires externally defined goals and reinforcements	Has self-defined goals and reinforcements
Needs organization provided	Can self-structure situations
More affected by criticism	Less affected by criticism
Uses spectator approach for concept attainment	Uses hypothesis-testing approach to attain concepts
Learns the concepts first then concentrates on details	Learns step-by-step
Likes to be introduced to information with humor and color	Adopts cumulative sequential pattern building towards a concept
Can work with distractors	Prefers quiet, well lit, formal design
Takes frequent breaks	Has a strong need to complete the task they are working on
Works on several tasks simultaneously; multi-tasks well	Responds well to words and numbers
Make up the majority of gifted children	Needs visual re-enforcement
Needs interesting lessons (to them)	Gives directions, fact sheets Underlines important sections
Discovers through group learning (small group techniques)	Provides feedback on details - in sequence
Needs written and tactual involvement	
Responds well to pictures	

Additionally, teachers, as individuals themselves, fall onto the same spectrum as their students. These attributes will be reflected in their teaching styles as is outlined in the following chart.

Teaching Styles

Field-Dependent/Global	Field-Independent/Analytical
Prefers teaching situations that allow interaction and discussion with students	Prefers impersonal teaching situations such as lectures Emphasizes cognitive aspects of instruction
Uses questions to check student learning when following instruction	Uses questions to introduce topics and following student answers
Uses student-centered activities	Uses teacher-organized learning situations
Viewed by students as teaching "facts"	Viewed by students as encouraging them to apply principles
Provides less feedback Avoids negative evaluation	Gives corrective feedback Uses negative evaluation as a teaching tool
Strong when establishing a warm and personal learning environment	Strong in organizing and guiding student learning

Finally, a list of suggestions is provided to motivate FI and FD students. Remember that all students fall somewhere on the spectrum of field dependent/independent learners. Some may appear to exhibit characteristics of both types, while others are more dominantly FD or FI. You will also notice that these suggestions can be implemented concurrently. Adjusting your teaching to assist your learners need not be a burden. It does not equate to thirty-two different lessons. It simply means incorporating elements into each lesson executed.

Motivating Students

Field-Dependent/Global	Field-Independent/Analytic
Use verbal praise	Through grades
Assisting the teacher	Participate competitively
External rewards (stars, stickers, prizes)	Give choices of activities Keep a personal goal chart
	Showing students the value of the task
Provide outlines and structure	Give them the freedom to design their own structures

Teaching Field Dependent/Global Students

Introducing the objective	Begin the lesson with a story, an anecdote or humor relating to the content. If possible, include the student's experiences or a realistic example.
Discovery through group learning	Avoid giving too many facts. These are discovered through small group interactions, such as: circle of knowledge, team learning, brainstorming, case study, etc.
Written and factual involvement	Create graphs, map, illustrate, draw, role-play, charts, invent games, make things, etc. Observe them as they develop teaching skills when they have to teach other students, especially affective with using computers.

Teaching Field-Independent/Analytic Students

Explanations and visual reinforcement	Analytics respond to key words and numbers. Write these on the board as you go. Answer questions about details directly. Include visual stimulation, such as the board and overheads.
Directions	List all relevant information regarding assignments, work requirements, objectives and directions on paper or have the students copy them from the board. Don't tell them; show them.
Step-by-step	Proceed step-by-step through the information needed to acquire skills. Write key words on the board. Underline important sections or use highlighters. Check homework daily. Teach independent use of the library facilities, etc. Ways to instruct other students, which often occurs when using computers.
Testing and feedback	Provide instant feedback on tests and assignments (as soon as possible). Do what you say you will do! Analytics hold you to your word.

To address all FD/Global and FI/Analytic Learners in the classroom, techniques for both groups need to be included in planning and executing instruction.

CASE STUDY 1
Learning Styles

Mr. Johnson is an effective 11th grade science teacher. He is usually well-prepared and has a reputation around the high school, as a "no-nonsense" teacher. Johnson clearly lays out the expectations for class each day. For the most part, everyone does what is expected. Everyone that is, except Tyrone, who continues to show Mr. Johnson he does not care. Under his breath, Tyrone says, "Here he goes again, acting like some tyrant, telling us what we have to do, I'm almost a grown man." Mr. Johnson has become accustomed to Tyrone's negative reactions to him. He's frustrated and knows Tyrone can do better than the consistent C's he earns in his class.

Mr. Johnson has had enough. He calls Tyrone out of the classroom for a conference. He begins lecturing Tyrone about the importance of school, and how these assignments are going to help him get in to college and to someday get a great job. Tyrone looks at him and says, "I'm a ball player, school work is not important to my getting paid."

Mr. Johnson is a true academic, he also teaches part time at the local community college. During his 8 years as a science teacher at the high school he seldom, if ever, attends after school activities. In actuality, he has strong views regarding ways extracurricular activities at the high school get in the way of learning.

Nonetheless, later that day, Mr. Johnson runs into the basketball coach at the high school. As is typical, Coach Jones invites Mr. Johnson to the game. As was customary, Mr. Johnson respectfully declines, but decides to ask him if he knows Tyrone. Coach responds, "Yes, he's one of my team captains and a natural leader. The other players actually listen to him and no one works harder. "

The bell rings and the two depart before Mr. Johnson could express his concerns. As the coach leaves, he yells, "We will finish talking later, are you sure you can't make the game? I'm sure Tyrone would be excited to see you. It would be like having another coach on the court."

Questions for Reflection

1. What do you feel is occurring between Mr. Johnson and Tyrone?

2. What can Mr. Johnson do to connect better with Tyrone?

3. Why does Tyrone simply complete enough assignments to get by in Mr. Johnson's class?

4. Based on the case study, do you think Tyrone is a field dependent or field-independent learner?

5. Based on the conversation with the coach, what teaching and learning strategies could Mr. Johnson use to engage Tyrone?

REFERENCES

Cognitive Style - Field-dependence and Field-independence. (n.d.). *In Social Issues Reference online*. Retrieved from http://social.jrank.org/pages/147/Cognitive-Style-Field-Dependence-Field-Independence.html.

Gardner, H. (1983). *Frames of Mind: The Theory of Multiple Intelligences*. New York: Basic Books Inc.

Guild, P. (1994). The culture/learning style connection. *Educational Leadership, 51(8)*, 16-21.

Guild, P. B., & Garger, S. (1985). *Marching to different drummers*. Alexandria: Association for Supervision and Curriculum Development.

Guisande, M., Paramo, M., Tinajero, C., & Almeida, L. (2007). Field dependence-independence (FDI) cognitive style: An analysis of attentional functioning. *Psicothema, 19(4)*, 572-577.

Kolb, D. (1983). *Experiential learning: Experience as the source of learning and development*. Upper Saddle River: Prentice Hall, Inc.

Ku, D., & Soulier, J., (2009). The effects of learning goals on learning performance of field-dependent and field-independent late adolescents in a hypertext environment. *Adolescence, 44(175)*, 651-664.

CHAPTER 8
Stages of Cultural Identity

The world's greatest problems do not result from people being unable to read and write. They result from people in the world—from different cultures, races, religions, and nations—being unable to get along and to work together to solve the world's intractable problems. (Banks, 2004, p. 291)

James Banks (2004) developed a six-stage model of cultural identity. Understanding the stages of cultural identity is valuable when assessing students' needs as well as in determining the best methods to use for instruction. Each of the stages describes the way an individual views the world and their place within it. Practical applications for addressing each stage's existence in the classroom environment will be discussed. For each stage, the suggestions given are intended to assist students in progressing from their current stage to the next stage of identity development. The ultimate goal is to produce students who are able to live, work and interact with others, representing a global society.

Stage One: Cultural Psychological Captivity

During the first stage, an individual believes in the negative ideologies and beliefs about his or her cultural group which are institutionalized within the mainstream society. Individuals become ashamed of his or her cultural group and identity. Researchers (Banks, 2004) state that some individuals who are members of historically victimized groups through discrimination, such as Polish Americans, the deaf, the blind, and gays, as well as members of highly visible and stigmatized racial groups, such as African Americans, and Chinese Canadians, are likely to experience a form of cultural psychological captivity.

In order for individuals such as students, to progress from this stage to the next, they must spend time exploring their own personal cultural identity. Experiences that allow them to discover more about the realities of their culture, assist in shifting from a place of captivity into the next stage in which they can see the positives of their culture, the way their culture exists and the way their culture contributes to the greater environment in which they live. Fears and negative images are addressed, explained, and processed so that the student may move from the stage one negative perspective to one of more understanding and acceptance.

> **Stage One Example:**
>
> Students are given a project in which they must choose a holiday which is important in their culture. If they are unsure, they may ask a parent or family member. The student will create a poster with the major elements of the holiday displayed. The poster must include the origins of the holiday as well as current places in the world other than their home country where the holiday is also celebrated. Students will present the poster to the class and discuss the important components of their family's holiday.

Stage Two: Cultural Encapsulation

During the Cultural Encapsulation stage, individuals retreat and begin to become defensive of their culture identity. The retreat is voluntary and the individual begins to believe that his/her culture is superior to other groups. As the title suggests, the individual encapsulates themselves within their cultural group and can become very exclusive in their actions and associations. Many times this stage is characterized by negative and hostile feelings toward other cultures.

Moving from this stage to the next requires knowledge of other cultures encountered by the individual. Individuals limit their involvement in their own cultural activities. Through education, the negative and hostile feelings espoused by the individual are lessened. They then move to a more positive outlook on the relationship between different cultures within larger society. Activities and assignments that encourage comparing and contrasting different elements of cultures assist in diminishing the negative stereotypes and creating new realities for students.

Stage Two Example:

Students are asked to look at an element of their culture, such as religious customs, marriage ceremonies, dress, food, holidays, music or dance, and compare the element to the same element found in another culture. The research must be balanced and accurate and the product must visually reflect that balance, ie. Venn diagram or t-chart comparison. In some cases, it will be necessary for the teacher to explain instances where biases and opinions cloud the accuracy of the product.

Stage Three: Cultural Identity Clarification

This stage brings a higher level of understanding and acceptance of a student's own cultural group. In this stage, individuals are able to clarify their personal attitudes and their cultural identities to reduce intra-psychic conflict and to develop clarified positive attitudes toward his or her cultural group. The student learns self-acceptance; thus, developing the characteristics needed to accept and respond more positively to outside cultural groups. During this stage, the individual can accept and understand both the positive and negative attributes of his or her cultural group. Through educational experiences, the student learns not only about their own cultural group, but also other cultures.

Moving from this stage to the next requires more focused study of other ethnic and racial groups. Using lessons comparing different cultural groups with respect to specific topics will develop a deeper understanding of how those communities function and the similarities that lie between different cultures. Experiential exercises can be powerful in this transition as students evaluate their understanding of the experiences they have. It is important that students feel safe to express their opinions with the instructor providing effective guidance when such opinions might be negative or unfounded. These conversations will allow students to gain a new perspective and learn through the overall process.

Stage Three Example:

Members of different cultural communities, who live in the same area as the school, are invited to share their culture with the class. Coordinate the visits so that more than one culture presents their information on the same day. Students are required to pre-formulate questions to ask. After the presentations, debrief students so that they can express their opinions and verbally process the learning experienced through these presentations.

Stage Four: Biculturalism

During this stage, individuals develop a healthier sense of cultural identity and the psychological characteristics and skills needed to participate successfully in his/her own cultural community as well as in another culture's community. The individual's perspective changes, as they are able to view events and situations through a new lens. Individuals in this stage seek out cultural experiences and enjoy traveling within different cultural groups. They have developed a skill set which allows them to "code switch" and feel comfortable among individuals representing different cultures. Traditionally, many marginalized groups function on this level as they attempt to blend in with the dominant culture, yet maintain the culture of their origins.

As with the previous stage, experiential exercises are a powerful way to move students further in their biculturalism to a state of multiculturalism. As the individual moves into stage five, this implies an ability to function within different cultural groups in a variety of situations, even those which might be unique for that culture. Providing students with such experiences will help to acclimate them and allow them to function effectively in future instances.

> **Stage Four Example:**
> Take the students on a field trip for a cultural experience such as multicultural fair, a religious ceremony, a community event, etc. Require students to record their observations and compare what they saw and experienced with their own cultural norms and practices. As with all experiential exercises, communicate with parents regarding the goals and purpose for the trip. Thoroughly debrief the students regarding this experience.

Stage Five: Multiculturalism and Reflective Nationalism

In stage five, the individual develops a clear, reflective, positive, personal, cultural and national identity reflecting the actual self. In this stage, individuals are able to function beyond superficial levels within several cultural groups in their own country. They understand the symbols, customs and practices of multiple cultures and feel comfortable around different groups. An individual within this stage can perceive the impact that events and policies have on multiple ethnic and cultural communities and typically embraces a much more inclusive multi-cultural position.

Moving from National Multiculturalism to a more global cultural perspective requires the student to also have a global knowledge of many concepts, from politics to economics to social issues around the world. Encouraging students to become involved in organizations such as Model U. N. will allow them to explore different topics that would be relevant to multiple cultural groups. These types of organizations also require students to view issues from different perspectives, such as the perspective of an Eastern European or African country, rather than that of the United States.

Stage Five Example:

Model United Nations is a powerful strategy for educating students about current events, international topics, diplomacy and the mission of the United Nations. Students research global issues facing different cultures within their countries. Conferences and meetings require students to identify with a country and argue critical issues from that country's perspective.

Stage Six: Globalism and Global Competency

Individuals within Stage Six have a reflective, clean and positive cultural, national and global identity with regard to knowledge, skills, attitudes, and abilities needed to function within cultures inside his or her own nation, as well as within cultures in other parts of the world. This stage encompasses all that is described within stage five, but adds the element of a global community. This person functions as one who is a part of every culture. This person has internalized the ethical values and principals considered universal and has developed the skills to actualize their commitments within the greater global community. There is a level of balance within these individuals that is unparalleled as they are able to effectively move within and between cultures in a respectful and effective way.

There is a difference between a traveling foreigner and a foreign traveler. A traveling foreigner studies the culture, art, religion, and people in an act of being in the culture and understanding it. The foreign traveler retains his own culture learning nothing of the one he visits. He is brass, bold and ethnocentric. The question is not which one is right or wrong, but simply, which one are YOU? (Submitted by an SIE 06-07 student, who saw this written on a graffiti wall of a youth hostel in Spain.) (Pederson, 2009, p. 82)

Each of the six stages discussed can also be found within the staff of any given school. So, although suggestions are given primarily for instructing students in each of the stages and moving them forward to a state of deeper cultural awareness, it is equally important, if not more so, that administrators, teachers and support staff understand and work to improve upon their current stage of identity. Consider the following scenario:

Ms. Chang is a Chinese American high school algebra teacher. She is extremely proud of her heritage. She shops only at Asian owned stores, follows current Chinese fashion closely and is very vocal about the superiority of her race. She does not associate with other members of the staff who are not Asian. She has been known to give higher grades to her Asian students and has frequently been heard saying disparaging remarks about her African American students. She has stated more than once that African American students are not good at math and should never be made to take anything higher than pre-Algebra. As a result of her teaching style and comments, many parents have begun to complain and request that their students be removed from the class.

This example shows a staff member who is in Stage Two: Cultural Encapsulation, on the cultural identity spectrum. Ms. Chang's superiority complex is affecting the achievement of her students. Prejudices such as these create an environment where the students are not given the opportunity to succeed. The teacher feels that his or her efforts are wasted on the student because they (the teacher) have a preconceived notion that the student cannot perform due to his or her race or ethnicity. This is also directly related to the Pygmalion Effect.

> Even in the face of new encounters, teachers' views are often reinforced instead of dispelled, as our minds will overlook contrary data to find the "evidence" necessary to support our views.

CASE STUDY 1
Stages of Cultural Identity

Mr. Frederick is a European American English teacher working at an inner city middle school. He is very well traveled, having visited over 25 different countries. He speaks 4 different languages and loves to decorate his classroom with treasures collected from his travels.

In the first three weeks of the new school year, Mr. Frederick likes to have the class participate in a number of activities to help them get to know one another and become more comfortable with their environment. One of the activities involves the class first identifying their own heritage, then reading about different cultures and making a comparison to their culture. During the activity, the following exchange takes place:

Marissa (African American female): "I don't see what the big deal is about White people. They can't dance as well as Black people; they aren't as pretty; and they can't play sports. Black people are much better at all of the things that really matter."

Shae (African American female): "You aren't embarrassed by the drop-out rate of Black people? I think it's horrible. Why can't we succeed and make money like the White people?"

Hector (Hispanic male): "You think you have it bad, Mexicans are blamed for all kinds of crime and half of us never even make it to college. I wish I was White."

Lucy (Hispanic female): "You guys have obviously not watched the news or paid attention to pop culture and politics. There are tons of famous and successful African Americans and Hispanic Americans. The key is to learn about each other's cultures and be able to move successfully through different situations experienced by various cultures."

Mr. Frederick: "That is a really good point, Lucy. As you guys read about these new cultures, let's compare them to your own and see if we are really that different. Each of you are important individuals who have the potential to do great things... what will you do with your life?"

Questions for Reflection:

1. Identify the stage of cultural identity for each person in the case study.

2. How does Lucy's perspective differ from Marissa's?

3. What impact do you think Mr. Frederick's background has on the perceptions of the class?

4. Do you think Mr. Frederick will be able to help advance any of these students to a new level of cultural identity? Why or why not?

REFERENCES

Banks, J.A. (2004). Teaching for social justice, diversity, and citizenship in a global world. *The Educational Forum, 68,* 289-298.

Banks, J. A. (2006). *Cultural Diversity and Education: Foundations, Curriculum, and Teaching.* Boston: Allyn and Bacon.

Pederson, P. (2009). Teaching toward and ethno-relative world view through psychology study abroad. *Intercultural Education, 20(1),* S73-S86.

CHAPTER 9
Cultural and Social Capital

Theoretical Framework

Consider the students whom you have encountered who just seem to "get it." Concepts come easily to them and often they are able to make connections demonstrating a deeper understanding of the material. Compare those students to others who have difficulty grasping concepts even when these are presented using various types of strategies and from multiple angles. When you ask them to "think of a time when you...," they have no idea of how to begin. What is the difference between these students? Does it have to do with their ethnic background? Or does it have more to do with the experiences they are bringing to the classroom? Social and cultural capital theorists will argue that it is a little of both.

Social capital and cultural capital are two terms referring to the skills and encounters a person has experienced, which can lead to their success in life. In this chapter, both terms, social capital and cultural capital, will be explored individually along with their implications for education.

Cultural Capital

Cultural capital is a theory first presented by Pierre Bourdieu in the 1970s, as a way to explain the social inequalities existing between groups due to their cultural skills, knowledge and abilities. Since its proposal, cultural capital has been scrutinized and has evolved (1973). In this chapter, two definitions of this theory will be examined: highbrow, cultural capital and contextually valued cultural capital.

Highbrow cultural capital centers around the notion that cultural capital as the acquisition of "highbrow" cultural knowledge and competence; basically the more knowledgeable you are and the more experiences you have with what is considered mainstream culture in the community in which you reside, the more cultural capital you possess (Winkle-Wagner, 2010). Mohr and DiMaggio (1995) considered factors such as parental economic status and education when measuring the upward mobility of students and ethnic groups. Their research asserted that participation in the cultural activities of the mainstream upper class, such as visiting museums, attending classical music concerts, art galleries and plays, and vacationing leads to academic success and increased college potential. "By cultural capital, we refer to prestigious tastes, objects, or styles validated by centers of cultural authority, which maintain and disseminate societal standards of value and serve collectively to clarify and periodically revise the cultural currency" (Mohr & DiMaggio, 1995, p. 168).

Mohr and DiMaggio's (1995) work, as well as studies conducted by other scholars in the field, indicated that cultural capital played a large role in success as students completed K-12 education and moved on to college and a career. The knowledge of the experiences of upper class culture contributed to higher standardized test results, admission into college and even influenced the types of colleges which students pursued for admission. Results showed an increased competency in activities involving critical thinking, writing skills and knowledge pertaining to the humanities, such as art, history and sociology.

However, the ability of students to process and apply what was learned and experienced through the cultural capital acquisition failed to be explained. In other words, simply going to the theater or viewing fine art exhibits is insufficient to affect academic performance per se. Though processing the information through discussion and application, served to solidify the cultural capital attained (Winkle-Wagner, 2010).

An alternate yet related form of cultural capital is contextually valued cultural capital. This type of cultural capital allows for different types of cultural capital, which are valuable in various situations. This model reveals that all students possess cultural capital. The difference is whether or not the particular cultural capital possessed is considered valuable in a given situation (Winkle-Wagner, 2010). The cultural capital brought to the classroom by students representing different ethnic groups through sharing their customs, traditions, ideals and experiences have not been discounted. However, in the mainstream White culture, much of that type of cultural capital is not valued. Therefore, students possessing a rich, ethnic cultural capital, find difficulty in advancing because they fail to possess the "right kind" of cultural capital.

Social Capital

"[Social Capital is] the networks, trust, norms and values that enable individuals and organizations to achieve mutual goals" (Dhillion, 2009, p. 692). Social capital differs from cultural capital in that it refers to relationships an individual makes both inside and outside of his or her ethnic group. These networks act as ways of gaining entrance into more specific communities. Resources gained through these connections can ultimately be combined and utilized to create economic and social opportunities for the individuals involved. Social capital can affect the potential for upward mobility in both a positive and negative way. Social connections and networks may be beneficial for one goal, yet detrimental to another (Abada & Tenkornag, 2009).

As with cultural capital, individuals from the mainstream dominant culture typically have a distinct advantage in gaining social capital.

Their social position automatically gives them a boost in social status. Immigrants and children of immigrants, however, have difficulty in gaining social capital. Trust plays a very big role in upward mobility. "Establishing these trustful relations is especially crucial for the children of immigrants, who also have to deal with their racial status, that is, their ascribed physical characteristics or skin color, which may hinder their upward mobility." (Abada & Tenkornag, 2009, p. 190) "Similarly, for the children of immigrants, relationships with network members can only be beneficial when they trust those relationships to provide useful information and support. These trustful relations extend to family members, role models, teachers, peers and their neighborhoods" (Schaefer-McDaniel, 2004, p. 162).

Implications for Education

The definition of contextually valued, cultural capital is especially pertinent as it deals with a person's perceptions of the values and experiences a student brings to the classroom. When teachers are unaware of the cultural background and experiences of their students, they are likely to make assumptions based on the students' behavior. This also occurs with students of poverty. Assumptions are made about a student's ability to obtain cultural capital due to their socio-economic status. As a result, the student may not have the opportunities to reach their full potential. "In other words, students' grades were indirectly affected by teachers' implicit judgments of a student's background and ability. Teachers' judgments were not necessarily based on skill or merit, but on perceptions of background" (Winkle-Wagner, 2010, p. 41).

Being aware of the involvement needed to increase a student's "highbrow" cultural capital, as defined by Mohr and DiMaggio (1995), is the first step in changing teaching habits and styles. Student participation in cultural activities in schools provides a better foundation for less economically fortunate students to gain cultural capital and therefore, become upwardly mobile. In essence, for those students who may be the first in their family to go to college and achieve a higher degree, the teacher becomes the parent figure and should assist the student in understanding the cultures to which they are exposed. Through these activities, the student is able to adequately process and internalize the information begin presented.

This idea is pertinent for social capital. For example, teachers of immigrant students or students who are first time college attendees, must teach their students to navigate the social networks necessary to succeed in the mainstream culture. This would include interviewing skills, professional etiquette, and proper dress along with other skills. Business, economics, theater, and speech courses are beneficial in teaching the elements of social awareness. As will be discussed in the next chapter, students learn by observation and example; therefore, the conduct and expectations of their superiors and role models is key.

CASE STUDY 1
Social and Cultural Capital

Pedro is a middle class, Hispanic junior at Glendale High School. Growing up, Pedro's parents worked hard to make sure he received a well-rounded education, both in and out of public school. When not in school, Pedro takes piano lessons and plays soccer. His mother loves going to museums and frequently drags Pedro along with her. For as long as he can remember, his dad has made sure he understood the importance of art and different genres of music. When Pedro took his SAT recently, he scored in the 95th percentile.

Jose lives down the street from Pedro and is also a junior at Glendale. Jose usually spends time after school playing video games and he also plays on the community soccer team. Both of his parents work full time and rarely take him anywhere out of the ordinary. He has a large family in El Salvador and keeps in touch with them via Skype and telephone calls. Jose also likes to spend time at the local cultural center. Whenever Pedro asks Jose if he wants to go to the theater with his family, Jose laughs and says, "No." When Jose took his SAT recently, he struggled with the vocabulary and scored in the 75th percentile.

Both students are preparing to begin their college search. They both have very different views on which college they want to attend. Pedro is considering a liberal arts college although his high SAT score and minority status, will give him the opportunity to attend an Ivy League School. Jose isn't really sure if he even wants to go to college. He thinks he'll probably go to community college or a trade school. His SAT scores are not high enough for the colleges in which he is interested. Futher, he failed to participate in extra-curricular activities while in high school. However, his experience volunteering at the local Hispanic Heritage Center has helped him gain connections for employment after high school.

Questions for Reflection

1. How is Pedro's upbringing an example of acquiring Cultural Capital?

2. In what way did the experiences Pedro have, contribute to his potential success after high school?

3. What could Jose have done differently to increase his Cultural Capital?

4. What kinds of activities can the school system support to assist students like Jose, whose parents may not be able to take them to 'highbrow' cultural activities?

5. What type of capital does Jose possess?

6. How might Jose's capital help him in the future?

REFERENCES

Abada, T., & Tenkorang, E. (2009). Pursuit of university education among the children of immigrants in Canada: The roles of parental human capital and social capital. *Journal of Youth Studies, 12(2)*, 185-207.

Bourdieu, P. (1986). The Forms of Capital. In J.G. Richardson (Ed.) *Handbook of Theory and Research for the Sociology of Education*, New York: Greenwood Press, pp. 241-258.

Dhillon, J. (2009). The role of social capital in sustaining partnership. *British Educational Research Journal, 35(5)*, 687-704.

Mohr, J., & DiMaggio, P. (1995). The intergenerational transmission of cultural capital. *Research in Social Stratification and Mobility, 14*, 167-199.

Schaefer-McDaniel, N. J., (2004). Conceptualizing social capital among young people: Toward a new theory. *Children, Youth and Environments, 14(1)*, 153-172.

Winkle-Wagner, R. (2010). Uses and abuses of cultural capital in educational research. *ASHE Higher Education Report, 36(1)*, 23-57.

CHAPTER 10
Symbolic Interactions Theory

Theoretical Framework

Symbolic Interactions Theory was first developed by University of Chicago faculty member, George H. Mead (1934), and later published by his student, Herbert Blumer (1969). Mead believed that the relationships and interactions occurring between the self, others and their environment create meaning and change for those interacting. It is through these interactions that people identify with and define their world. It is more than just responding to social and environmental cues; it is a process of building upon experiences and a growing knowledge of situations to effectively navigate the world (Blumer, 1969).

> *There are three main premises of symbolic interactionism: (a) human beings act on the basis of the meanings they ascribe to things in their environment, (b) these meanings arise out of the social interaction that one has with others and the society, and (c) these meanings are worked within an interpretative process used by the person in dealing with the environment. (Doherty & Craft, 2011, p. 67)*

Symbolic interactionism focuses on the ways people interact with each other through symbols. Symbols range from words and roles to gestures and rules. Each symbol helps place meaning on and create an understanding of situations. This meaning also must come from the social interaction with others. Meaning cannot be gained independently through individual experiences because we learn the value of things from the feedback of others (Vygotsky, 1978). From these experiences individuals construct an understanding of their world. This meaning and understanding of the world is not defined and static, rather it can change and evolve as different stimuli enter the environment.

Symbolic Interactionism and the Family

"Parents are the most significant environmental force in a child's life and play an indispensable role in his or her development..." (Colarusso, 1992, p. 5). From the lens of symbolic interactionism, the family is a unit of interacting personalities. As a social group, the family greatly influences the development of a child's self-concept and ways they interact with their environment. We are not born knowing how the world and society functions. However, from infancy, children learn the structure of society through their interaction with other humans. They learn very quickly who holds positions of power and authority, who provides safety, security and sustenance, and who can be trusted. As children grow, their perception of the world is shaped by the situations they encounter. Additionally, children learn how to respond to situations by observing others in similar situations.

One of the most important things that children gain from their interactions with people and situations is their self-concept. Self-concept is primarily shaped by ways others treat us, especially those who are of importance, such as parents, friends, and

> Every school should have a strategic parental involvement plan that includes best practices in parenting and facilitating a home environment that nurtures the whole child.

teachers. Self-concept is fluid. A child can have a negative self-concept when they are young due to negative interactions with adults and peers; however, later in life the same student can develop a positive self-concept resulting from interactions with positive influences (Plunkett, 2008).

Every school should have a strategic parental involvement plan that includes best practices in parenting and facilitating a home environment that nurtures the whole child.

Implications for Education

As per the *Symbolic Interactionism Theory*, knowing and understanding the symbols of the students' world is fundamental for educators' continued training. "As the child moves out of the nuclear family and into the community, environmental factors become broader based and include the influence of teachers, neighbors, peers and coaches and the like" (Colarusso, 1992, p. 5).

Using symbols with which students in our classrooms interact assists teachers in instruction. Not only must schools and classrooms seek to mirror the symbols students experience in their everyday lives, teachers must seek to challenge the misinterpretations that students may have gained through negative relationships.

Rather than information being imparted from teacher to students, the teacher's role now requires instructors to guide students in learning how to think critically and process beneficial information (Bastable, Gramet, Jacobs, & Sopczyk, 2011). For those students who have experienced a turbulent childhood, experienced teachers who failed to believe in them, or who experienced absentee parents, learning these life skills is necessary for continuing their education.

Further, symbolic interactionism highlights the importance of teachers serving as a role model for students. The key to this theory is the interaction that occurs between the individual and other people as a way of interpreting situations and creating an understanding of the world. Thus, positive role models, such as teachers, can have a profound influence on a child's world-concept and self-concept.

In addition to the relationship building opportunity present in this theory, teachers can also find ways to better motivate and teach their students by understanding their symbols. A theme throughout this book has been the importance of understanding our students' backgrounds so that we may meet them at their level of progress and assist them in reaching their potential. Students are more likely to comprehend and retain the concept knowledge when they are taught through symbols with which they are familiar. By learning the "language" of the students, the symbols they use and the value they place on them, teachers can better frame their lessons in a context students will be able to understand and apply.

CASE STUDY 1
Symbolic Interactions Theory

Amber Cole is a 14-year old girl, who was filmed giving oral sex to a teenage boy right outside the doors of their high school during the middle of the day. As Amber performed this sexual act, she had two spectators. One who was video recording and another, who was watching and was recorded as the witness. The video was very explicit and did not hold back any footage despite the obvious location.

The three boys involved, as the video director, audience and boy receiving the oral sex, decided that they wanted to share their "work" with the world. They wanted to be known as the big shots of the school. They posted the video on the social network, "Twitter." Once posted, it would be expected that Amber would respond with shame or embarrassment. Initially, she didn't. She decided to create a "Twitter" account to exploit her video even more. Amber began to grow into an overnight sensation and for the wrong reasons. She bragged about what she did and did everything she could to increase her Twitter "followers."

When asked why she would allow this sort of thing to happen she tweeted (sent a message via twitter), that she wanted to be like her role models. She then went on to name her role models as being Kim Kardashian, Lil' Kim and Trina. She claimed that these were the positive examples of women she knew. They were beautiful, famous and rich and this is what she aspired to be. This was her only interaction of what a successful woman was and they all made it by exploiting their sexuality.

Soon Amber's Twitter account began to receive millions of derogatory slurs, remarks and personal favors. People became so vindictive toward Amber her perception on what was fame turned into misery. She began to threaten suicide and speak horribly about her familial circumstances. She became so overwhelmed with negativity that the "Twitter" organization was forced to shut down her account for fear of a liability lawsuit.

Questions for Reflection

1. Do you think that Amber missed out on "positive" symbolic interactions? If so, from what relationship? What about the boys involved?

2. As individuals, once we are aware of our life meanings/thoughts/ identity are we responsible for those who have not processed their meanings/thoughts/identity? For instance, if the boys in the video knew better than to act as they did, were they responsible for acting 'better?'

3. Are we responsible for making others aware of our language?

4. As educators, should we consider the media in learning the symbolic interactions of our students? Would the media even constitute a symbolic interaction?

5. What language, meanings and thoughts can we assume Amber and the boys learned from their foundational relationships? What may have been some of their symbolic interactions?

6. As an educational system, how should the school district handle this situation?

7. How would you assist Amber in handling this symbolic interaction?

REFERENCES

Bastable, S. B., Gramet, P., Jacobs, K., Sopczyk, D. (2011). *Health Professional as Educator: Principles of Teaching and Learning*. Sudbury: Jones & Bartlett Learning.

Blumer, Herbert. 1969. *Symbolic Interactionism: Perspective and Method*. Englewood Cliffs: Prentice-Hall.

Colarusso, C.A. (1992). *Child and Adult Development: A Psychoanalytic Introduction for Clinicians*. New York: Plenum Press

Doherty, W., & Craft, S. (2011). Single mothers raising children with "male-positive" attitudes. *Family Process, 50(1)*, 63-76

Mead, G. H. (1934). *Mind, Self, and Society*. Chicago: University of Chicago Press.

Plunkett, S. (2008). *Symbolic Interactionism Theory* [word document]. Retrieved from http://www.csun.edu/~whw2380/542/542%20Reading%20and%20Lecture%20Notes.htm

Vygotsky, L.S. (1978). *Mind and Society: The Development of Higher Mental Processes*. Cambridge: Harvard University Press.

CHAPTER 11
Conclusion

Culturally responsive teaching is not something that comes easily. As is shared in this book, it is a learned skill set. This skill set has nothing to do with your ethnicity as an individual. These tools are motivated by the heart of the teacher, and their relentless commitment to unwrapping their self and views to bring about the powerful shifts necessary to create culturally responsive classrooms. Unfortunately, much of the needed information presented in this guide, is seldom part of teacher preparation programs.

I've worked with teachers all over the country and have experienced the frustration of educators desiring, but not knowing how, to respond appropriately to their students, especially their diverse population. As such, this book has been written to provide insight into and solutions for more effectively working with diverse learners.

As you read, you might have noticed that many of the theories apply to *all* learners, not only students of color or students from low socio-economic backgrounds. As such, use the knowledge gained through this book to create change where necessary for all students. As an equipped educator you have what you need to create the culturally responsive classroom you and your students deserve.

Remember, each and every child in America deserves a quality education. That means, as educators, we must figure out where they are, meet them there, and bring them to where they need to be. That also means, in many cases, that *we* must make some changes. Changes to our own mindset; possibly changes to our locus of control. In some cases, small adjustments to our teaching style and practices is all that is needed.

It has been my sincere desire that the theories explained within these pages have given you ample information with which to begin the process of creating a culturally responsive learning environment in which your students will thrive. But change must happen. Change is rarely easy, and it is often painful, but I guarantee that when you begin to respond in a culturally appropriate way to your students, you will be amazed at the results. The most difficult challenge is often unwrapping ourselves.

ABOUT THE AUTHORS

DR. TYRONE TANNER
primary author

 Dr. Tyrone Tanner is a Professor in the Educational Leadership Doctoral Program at Prairie View A & M University. He has 20 years of K-12 public school and higher education experience. His experience includes working with public schools as a consultant (with expertise in parenting, leadership, diversity, and urban school reform), high and middle school administrator, urban school personnel director, and middle and high school teacher.

Dr. Tanner's research has been published in more than 30 peer reviewed journals and he has written several books. He has presented his research in over 100 different venues. He currently serves as editor, associate editor, and editorial reviewer for multiple journals, and presents annually at numerous conferences and P-12 schools on topics such as teacher efficacy, building on the resiliency of learners, increasing parental involvement, and culturally responsive leadership. These workshops have proven to be effective in helping teachers work more successfully with diverse learners, as well as, increasing parental involvement.

Dr. Tanner received his Doctor of Education in Educational Leadership and Cultural Studies from the University of Houston, a Master of Education in School Administration and Supervision from Southern

University, and a Bachelor of Arts in Social Studies/Education from New-berry College.

Dr. Tanner's philosophy is firmly planted in the belief that all students can learn and if provided a culturally active classroom environment they can learn with exceptionality. He's committed and dedicated to developing a sense of self-efficacy by providing school educators and parents with the tools necessary to experience success with all children.

For consultations, products, and presentation scheduling for educators or parent workshops, please call 1-888-630-6650 or email Dr. Tanner directly at drtyronetanner@gmail.com.

MARY E. FRANK
contributing author

Mary E. Frank possesses a Master of Science in Teaching and has been an educator for more than ten years, serving as a social studies teacher, curriculum specialist and consultant. Working with diverse populations in the Houston Metropolitan area sparked an interest in learning more about the students whom she taught. She has seen, first hand, the effects of a culturally responsive classroom and the amazing academic achievement that can result. Mary is also the owner of Engaging Stations for Student Success, a product and service oriented company that provides engaging manipulatives and apps for the social studies classroom. Mary resides in California with her educator husband and their three children. For more information about Engaging Stations, visit www.engagingstations.com.